Plan for Hire
Choosing You in a Dead Economy

Forward

The time of this writing is late summer 2010. The sitting administration is hell-bent on reporting unemployment statistics below the psychological threshold of 10%. Numbers like 9.7%, 9.5%, 9.8% are spewed each day. Folding in marginally employed, those who are no longer accounted for courtesy of no longer looking, it's easy to reach figures in excess of 15%. Whatever the spin there is a lack of hiring – it's hard to imagine this changing for some time.

My goal is to provide you with a roadmap to find work – to help you find something that suits you and then give you the tools to prevail in an interview process; in some cases an interview that you create. The provided techniques will especially help you in slow times but will help you reach your goals in almost any market condition.

If you are out of work and looking, working but wish to change, hoping to get promoted, or simply recognize that you need to do something else, I can help.

My background working for and calling on public and private organizations has revealed new insight into creating and landing career opportunity. Using the methods presented in forthcoming pages will greatly improve your odds of being selected in traditional job search venues. The most important lesson I hope to demonstrate, however, is the potential for you to create an opportunity of your choosing - to leave you equipped with the tools for working with an organization creating a position that you help define. A position where you are the single candidate.

As a recent test-case for the methods presented herein, my wife decided to resume her career in 2010 after seventeen years staying at home to raise a family. Contemporary wisdom would have cast her as unemployable. Her skills were not "up-to-date", she was middle-aged, her absence from the workforce would raise eyebrows, and the unemployment picture as discussed was arguably over 10%. Lastly, her chosen field, aerospace, had been partially defunded under the Obama Administration. It took seven months from the time we formally began her search but she landed an engineering position with a top aerospace and defense company. Friends in the community were envious and a bit annoyed at her "luck". Seasoned people in the field were being let go as programs dried up. There were many capable and certainly more qualified candidates competing for work. What others didn't realize is that their traditional approach to finding work would no longer yield results - new times call for new measures.

I've learned so much in my career journey. Primarily I've learned how to sell an idea and follow through – you must deliver what you promise if your "stock" is to rise. There are winning tactics learned along the way that when executed will help you find and create job opportunities. I would like to share with you what I learned to make you more effective in your approach. Read on and my best of luck to you!

Chapter One – Background Discussion

This book assumes that you have been working in at least a quasi-professional capacity for a minimum of four years. Whether or not you have a college background is somewhat immaterial. If you are absolutely "green" to the working world you still may find useful information and approaches. My goal is to help you execute on a path you wish to pursue. Winning in the interview and subsequently in your job is not accidental. It's largely up to you to figure out what you want to do but once complete, I can help you prospect opportunities, get an interview, land a job, and advance.

Not mentioning the economic doldrums the U.S. is drifting through as of this writing (2010) would be negligent. I presume they will last for the next decade at least. Now that you are clearly not in an employee's market you need non-traditional help more than ever. Unlikely that a time will return when a pulse and no criminal background will get you started. Putting into practice the concepts I will share with you will place you ahead of your competition in any market. In times past the middle of the pack didn't have too much of an issue finding work. That may have changed forever.

I'd like to add that as far back as the late 1980s the notion of loyal employee equaling a steady career with good company started to fade. The mergers and acquisitions world exploded in the 1990s largely evaporating the concept of "fair" for most companies. Now in the second decade of the twenty-first century most companies will view you as a managed cost. Entry-level employment has usually been a hard sell but nothing like the present. Given the ebb-and-flow dynamics of today's workplace you will likely work for a minimum of four companies during your career. If you play it smart the changes will be your decision and allow you to advance.

Politics

Politics affect opportunities – your opportunities. Green jobs, Chief Diversity Officer, EEOC Attorney, working for the Office of

Communications and Outreach for the Department of Education, take note…every task that draws a salary and returns no material value to an economy must draw wealth from some portion of the economy that creates tangible material wealth. Titles originating from either direct legislation or in response to social pressure and/or political correctness typically do not positively impact GDP. Think about it. What is wealth? Homes, cars, tools, real estate, raw materials, food, apparel, energy, all that tangible stuff you can measure, own as property, trade, earn, and ultimately consume constitutes wealth - material wealth. In addition to tangible production there are many services that add value. Marketing, manufacturing consulting, banking, transportation planning, municipal services (provided by local governments) all arguably add value to the lives of others. I am not writing a book on spiritual well-being. I'm trying to help you find a job – I'm giving you the added bonus of offering guidance toward sustainable pursuits. Also, I need to provide some current economic background as the methods for landing a job as of this writing are in flux – obviously tactics change given a target organization and role.

As of late 2010 free enterprise is being called into question and challenged in unfamiliar ways. The future is unclear. It's likely, however, that anemic private sector hiring will be the rule going forward. Inasmuch as public jobs are parasitic to private enterprise and now are in greater proportion than they've ever been, I do not believe we will ever revisit a time when our economy is expanding so rapidly that good jobs are easy to find. As Americans we've allowed our federal and state governments to reach deeply into the free market. The concept of "free-market" has changed. As a rule bureaucracies do not shrink. They only grow. The public buys into a noble intent and in return reaps burdensome and costly rules that retard innovation and wealth creation.

While preaching the gospel of doom let me add the specter of currency collapse to this blue mosaic. Private business must earn the money it spends. This simple idea doesn't hold to government. It never did. Like a crack-habit-gone-wild the Fed needs deficit spending as its modus operandi and is positively incapable of balancing a budget. The trillions pledged away underscore more to follow. Remember this, as insular as Fed feels itself to be, there is no escaping market forces in the end. If not the debt, then the deficit at least will be remedied by printing money. Dollars in the post 2010 world will lose buying power on a large scale. I doubt foreign creditors will call in the debt as our fates are tied but I do think you will see diminished interest in our Treasury Bonds. The U.S. will either have to control spending and/or attempt to increase revenue. There is only one mode the Fed knows. Additional punitive tax burdens will follow adding to the drag on prospective growth.

Depressed yet? Don't be. Once you've written to your elected representatives turn your focus toward your career. True, low unemployment, rapid GDP growth, and frenzied hiring may be history but economic activity will not cease. Where posting on Monster.com and dialing up a headhunter or two used to suffice you now need a new battle plan. Career mobility will still exist. Society will not grind to a halt. There will be successful people always. What will change is demand. A few specific fields will play well into the hands of a perspective employee but very few. By and large requisitions for additional labor will be scarce. Competition will be hideous. In some way you will need to differentiate. Years will pass before some get the hang of "selling themselves" effectively. You will want to be tactical in your choice of education and career pursuits for certain but absolutely you will want to outsell your competition – get used to thinking of other applicants in that manner.

In using examples of parasitic tasks I hinted at the kinds of things I would encourage you to think about in your career planning. Some things to ask yourself; 1) Does your career path materially enhance the lives of others? 2) Is what you do heavily dependent on policy decision? 3) Do you foresee a growing or waning need for the services your career provides? The sharp growth of government jobs under President Obama is simply not sustainable. By contrast, whatever future-world looks like, we have a power grid that is about tapped out. There will be a wave of retirement in the electrical engineering field specific to power systems. This is one example of a field you might wish to pursue. Other fields likely to present demand include the traditional engineering fields, anything related to food distribution and agriculture, some branches of medicine (how the new Health-Care debacle will effect this is not clear yet), auto repair, and HVAC service and repair. Fields likely to remain weak for many years after Obama include: Heavy manufacturing, commercial construction, residential construction, leisure travel, restaurant and entertainment, luxury goods, durable goods, automotive, appliance, and mining.

Misuse of money largely by the U.S. Federal Government, the European Union, and U.S. consumers will lead to either a slow-growth economy or even a period of contraction. At the consumer level there will be less need (or inability to pay) for new stuff with an emphasis on fixing existing stuff and making it last through its economically useful life. A car, for example, might now need to last twenty years instead of a new one every five. The "McMansions" will no longer be built en masse. Think instead, a "dumbing down" of wants. Essentials will move at a good clip. Luxuries will hit a wall. Look for good performance in gardening, home repair, appliance/auto/electronic repair, infrastructure, internet movies, grocery stores, basically with less money people are going to spend more time close to home and trimming their entertainment budgets.

Enough prognostication – the important point is your opportunities will shift. Your approach to available opportunity will require change. You will want to consider creating opportunity – it's a path most of us never considered. Answering posted ads with cover letters and resumes while expecting to "hear back" is foolish today. Tomorrow it will be moronic. The following chapters equip you in approaching opportunity. More importantly I will teach you to create your own opportunity – enjoy!

Organizations

Types of employers are nearly infinite. The majority of us, however, draw our pay from public companies, private companies, the federal government, state and local governments, and non-profit organizations. Below, I provide somewhat simplistic, yet potentially useful constructs.

Employer type one – large publicly held company:

Generalizations

Pluses:

- ❖ Relatively stable. Able to withstand economic turmoil.
- ❖ Flexible work hours.
- ❖ Accommodating, good "work-life balance".
- ❖ Well-known – likely a good resume reference.
- ❖ Loose hierarchy.
- ❖ Good financial stability.
- ❖ Absence of nepotism.
- ❖ EEOC compliant – diverse workforce opportunities.
- ❖ At least mid-level compensation.

Minuses:

- ❖ Bureaucratic.
- ❖ Hire and fire easily based on market conditions with the exception that HR stymies the hiring process.
- ❖ Impersonal, lots of "fat" – being somewhat bureaucratic there are many jobs not connected with value-stream.
- ❖ For those who enjoy greater risk-reward structure there is potentially less opportunity.
- ❖ Heavy "Office politics".
- ❖ Glacial advancement pace.
- ❖ Shareholder versus customer dilemma. Lose focus on customer easily.

❖ Lots of time engaged in useless crap such as sensitivity training.
❖ Nothing gets done without the legal department signing off.
❖ Little rapid-growth potential.

Additional – working for a large publicly held corporation is not a bad feature on your resume. In fact, there is much benefit. Until you learn the workings of a Fortune 500 type company it's hard to know how to navigate a large organization to sell products/services effectively or advance your career. Oddly, things such companies do poorly open opportunity for someone else (i.e. consultants). Learn to navigate and you're closer to having this additional possibility near retirement. For those who like to avoid strict scrutiny and live somewhat in "the abyss" many fortune 500 companies offer a degree of anonymity shared with the likes of government employment. With all the talk of "lean-and-mean" many large publicly held companies waste as much time and money as public sector employment. You too can earn a decent salary and accomplish little meaningful work if that is your wish. However, if the opposite is your ambition you may have a hard time getting noticed for the right things. Standing out in a large publicly held corporation usually requires having the right advocate(s).

How they hire – companies of this profile will seek candidates using head-hunters, web-based registration, internal references, campus recruitment, and job-fairs to gather profiles for a candidate database. Typically department managers will need to argue for a requisition approval to add or replace staff. The same person will also need to draft a profile describing who they are looking for. Usually HR takes over for initial screening and provides the department manager with resumes of potential interviewees. Vetting "best value" with this approach is a bit of a crap shoot. Getting noticed through the typical routes is unlikely.

Giving yourself the edge – I echo a recurrent theme; you must bypass the recruitment malaise referenced above. It's more a screen than a tool. Skip it! Make yourself known to target general managers or directors. If you are vying for such a position yourself you need to introduce yourself to the next level…something along the lines of an executive V.P. Someone from the inside needs to be your advocate – the higher the reference the better your shot. Your introduction needs be concise…the contents: 1) Precisely how you can help. 2) Why you are the best choice. 3) You are available when and if an opportunity avails itself. You must sell your contact on what you can do for the department, company, etc. and show the tools to back it up. If you succeed, you have someone on the "inside" pulling for you. In today's climate there is almost no other way. I've made it sound simple. It's not. Forthcoming chapters will give you the how-to information.

Employer type two – small privately held company:

Generalizations:

Pluses:

- ❖ Pay scale not dictated by HR – it's between you and your boss.
- ❖ You get to wear many "hats". Your opportunity to learn/demonstrate multiple roles will never be as good.
- ❖ You have no choice but to make a great impact.
- ❖ Your work will greatly influence company profitability. Suppose you are a machinist and one CNC needs repair and is down for three hours…likely the owner will know.
- ❖ You are "noticed" by top management.
- ❖ If the company truly has good growth potential you will have a better chance to be buoyed along with the rise. You may one day be an executive of a large company.
- ❖ Related – you will develop close working relationships with current and future executives.
- ❖ Lack of bureaucracy – very much customer-focused.
- ❖ Related – company is necessarily "lean-and-mean".
- ❖ Understanding how you impact the fortunes of the company is easy.

❖ Benefits. I'm speaking here about an ownership stake as opposed to medical. There is little risk in asking for an equity stake at the right level. Minimal risk to the owner. The only drawback is that there are no shares issued hence it needs to be discussed in a percentage of equity.

Minuses:

❖ Nepotism rules…make sure if you are considering joining a similar company that sons and daughters won't be the de facto future executives. This needs to be understood going in.

❖ You are "noticed" by top management. Obviously this can work two ways.

❖ Sometimes ruled with the "iron fist", or at least the owner(s) has a say in every stinking thing. This can be the poster-child for micromanagement. If you are considering working for a company of this genre then do your homework to find out two things: 1) Is the owner focused on growth? 2) Does the owner understand they must relinquish control in order to grow? Typically a small private company hits that $50MM/year in sales point and there is a traditional impasse…the owner must let go to grow further. He/she cannot be involved in all decisions any longer. This is a tough line to cross for anyone.

❖ If you are using this as a reference no one knows who the hell you worked for.

❖ Only a minus for the lazy – if you plan on being a slug you won't make it here. Submit your resume for government or Fortune 500 employment...it's possible to find a home.

❖ Benefits. Now I'm referring to the traditional benefits. HR, using 100 employees as leverage, has little to bring into negotiations with the insurance companies et al. You might find 401K, insurance, flex-time, etc. lacking.

❖ Micromanaged atmosphere. The owner built this show. Maybe even the company name is his. Think you have open latitude to ply your trade? Not the place to do it – usually.

Additional – You can learn an incredible amount, you'll work your ass off, you can do so many things, and lastly you can learn every facet of a business. Name recognition will not be a plus if you want to move on. You'll have to be adept at telling your story. Hiring managers speak in terms of revenue you were responsible for and/or number of reports to counter claims that you held title in such a small shop. Typically a V.P. for a $20MM company is not on par with a Department Manager for a $20B company.

If you are intent on joining a small private company consider yourself getting married. You will need to be a better fit with the Management Team than otherwise. There is no switching to another department if things don't work out. You will work with these people for as long as you are with the company. If you do find this ideal coupling then the next hurdle is to sort truth from BS regarding growth goals. Every owner will reply "yes". Seldom does an owner (or owners) of a small private company have the grace to cede control necessary to grow. If that is already in the works and you can broker an ownership stake, then by all means, jump. The imperative is to understand what you are getting into. Large corporations and government employment offers more escape paths without having to find a new company.

How they hire – small private companies are generally less sophisticated in how they pursue candidates than larger bodies but they are exceptionally thorough in screening. They too know that the impact of one individual has the potential to be huge. "Culture" as viewed by stakeholders is critical beyond the Fortune 500 World. Look for trade-journal ads, newspaper ads, head-hunters, on-line, and to a degree, internal referrals. Word of note – small private companies tend not to engage in "HR paranoia". Chances are if there is an ad posted, they are looking to hire. Often in the larger corporate world, a selection has been made, but the posting is a compliance item. The interview process will generally begin and end with the owner(s).

Giving yourself the edge – selling your way in without a specific job opening is tougher with this crowd for one reason and easier for another. Clearly, adding staff is done rarely unless the company is outperforming the market. On the plus side, if you have talent they need that can supplant consulting fees while working needed functions you have a strong selling point. Large organizations are replete with disparate talent and much less sensitive to capability voids. Clearly such small companies are less visible and finding out they exist takes research.

If they are advertising an open role and you do get an "in" via one of the mentioned channels your edge is gained in the same way I will preach throughout the book. You will need to research the market, learn how you can further their goals, and tell the story from front to finish. It's o.k. to make a few assumptions too. Provide a detailed plan without coming across arrogant.

Employer type three – federal/state/local government:

Generalizations:

Pluses:

- ❖ Stable…at least perceived as such. Funding issues are usually levied against contractors. You are "Teflon" in many respects as a direct employee.
- ❖ Diverse workforce. Where else can a pre-op transgender with one leg and lisp have a de facto advantage?
- ❖ Flexible hours and lots of holidays.
- ❖ In certain venues performance demands are nil. Show up, be present and perform your duties in a perfunctory manner and you will remain employed forever…at least that's how the story goes. As a customer it certainly seems consistent.
- ❖ Largest employment base of all…over 2MM employed in 2010.
- ❖ Great benefits.

Minuses:

- ❖ Viewed unfavorably by the private sector. Real or imagined with a long track-record in government service the thought is you cannot last in a performance-driven culture.
- ❖ Bureaucratic.
- ❖ Lengthy application process.
- ❖ Not profitability driven.
- ❖ Your pay, while stable, is governed by the general schedule (GS). You will have steady but not dynamic compensation.
- ❖ Ample opportunity for non value-added positions…if true budget cuts ever materialize there will be ample opportunity for losing your job.
- ❖ Highly political…duh!
- ❖ Unions are the norm – American Federation of Government Employees (a.k.a. AFL-CIO). This is not a good thing folks…the impetus for forming unions was noble but they've largely outlived their use.

Additional – As of 2010 the United States Federal Government employed roughly two million workers. State and local governments employed yet more at over nine million. There are opportunities to find work. Not including the U.S. Military and the United States Postal Service, there is rapid growth in many federal functions including regulatory and educational pursuits. In times of economic turmoil the number of applicants also increases exponentially given applicant's draw to perception of stable employment in the public sector. The nation's largest union presence rests now in the government sector.

How they hire – I will mostly limit this discussion to the United States Federal Government as local governments vary. Let me begin by saying that the process requires patience and it is a process. My research-and-present-the-benefits approach may work in the latter phases of the interview process but there is virtually no way to circumvent a long and grueling application process to address a government opportunity. I refer you to www.usajobs.com and www.govtjobs.com. Not all agencies advertise positions on either. You are well advised to investigate which agency holds your interest and visit that website.

Giving yourself the edge - count on a long application process. Generally in the 6 – 18 month range if everything goes well. Connections count very little for your garden-variety roles. In this venue there are tricks of the trade. For example, initial screenings are somewhat mechanical involving the use of computer review or review by more government workers. Keywords are critical. Read the ad. Pull key words from the description and pepper your resume accordingly. Always craft versions of your resume relevant to each role you are applying for. The Fed uses a rating system of 1 – 100. Military service, disabled vet status, volunteer work, and other venues give you a nice boost. Your resume may be multiple pages but try to contain it to fewer than three. Understand that in this world you have potential employers who are less concerned with P&L performance than in the private sector - fiscal prudence is not required. If you really want job security focus on anything under Health and Human Services, Social Security, or anything exempt from appropriations. Department of Defense is subject to appropriations and highly dependent upon views of a sitting administration.

Interviews will be in panel format. Government HR processes resemble political-correctness on steroids. Each facet of the hiring process will be replete with steps to ensure objectivity and proper representation of diversity. It's o.k. and advisable to focus on what you've achieved. Consistent with all communications in written and spoken form you need to highlight accomplishment. In a government world you may want to slant your message toward "team building", project management, "collaboration", cost-savings, and stay away from revenue generation and profit (how sad is that?). Forgive the author intrusion here but to work for the Federal Government requires at least a temporary lobotomy in matters capitalist. To the extent profitability implies viability many government services are necessarily blind yet their rejection thereof is largely political. I ask you to simply be aware to boost your chances of joining up.

Employer type four – non-profit organizations:

Jettison the misnomer…non-profit pays! They just can't show a profit in order to maintain their tax-exempt status. What they don't spend directly toward their mission they must pay in salaries, advertising, improvements, etc. to avoid showing profit. Non-profit organizations are assumed to offer lower salaries than the private sector as workers are thought to be driven in part by altruistic motives. The salary gap has been closing.

Generalizations:

Pluses:

- ❖ Potentially fulfilling in ways beyond money. If you are indeed passionate about a certain cause, this venue can offer fulfillment beyond a more transactional organization.
- ❖ Gain notoriety. If you work your way to an officer level position in the right organization, you will interact with many organizations. Call it excellent networking.
- ❖ Not typically command-and-control organizations. Every voice is heard.
- ❖ Not heavily layered. Not too many levels between anyone and the CEO.
- ❖ Fund-raising is crucial but other factors weigh in judging success.
- ❖ Flexible hours, good work-life balance.

Minuses:

- ❖ Typically you will receive at least slightly less pay for similar private or government role.
- ❖ Difficult to join.
- ❖ As the economy wanes so do contributions.
- ❖ Highly political…to get and retain employment.

❖ Incredible energy spent soliciting funds…there is no other way – that is the lifeblood.

❖ If you are results and/or project oriented you may be disappointed. The direct tie between your efforts and organizational success can seem elusive in this environment.

❖ Limited advancement opportunity. Not many layers…this can be "good" yet if moving up the ladder is your thing there aren't many rungs here.

Additional – finding solid employment data for 2009/2010 was difficult at best. Suffice it to say there were about 1.5 million organizations in the U.S. having tax-exempt status at the time of this writing. Public charities make up about half of these organizations followed by roughly 42% non-profit organizations, and roughly 8% private foundations.

Attorneys, Program Managers, CFO, CEO, Campaign Director, and Finance Manager represent many of the executive titles you will see in non-profits. Obviously there has to be considerable accounting, fundraising, and promotion/advertising for non-profits. Related disciplines may find opportunity. There are even such titles as "Director of Major Gifts".

How the hire – nonprofit organizations do follow traditional paths to seek especially executive personnel. Understand, though that the organizations are flat and adding headcount is rare. Nonprofits will solicit input from board members, staff, community members, and even look to competitors to find candidates when the need arises. Generally it is a challenge to fill executive level positions but there is a line for staff positions…they have to compete with the private and public sectors for top management.

Giving yourself the edge – if you've volunteered for the target organization you have an in. Consider my earlier comment…if you're not vying for an executive level position you will have a tough row to hoe. In this case you will want to network as in no other venue. That will be your way in. Simple strategy – identify a handful of nonprofits in your area that you want to work with. Research each and articulate (on paper) why you want to work for each and what you will do for each. Ultimately how are you going to further the mission for each? Know it, believe it, and rehearse it so when you get your chance to tell your story you can be persuasive. Next, find out who the board members are for the target nonprofits. Call them and introduce yourself. Most often you will be politely referred to someone who will consider your resume etc. If you are willing to volunteer your time initially, then you may find a more willing reception. This is a long-term proposition. Unlikely you will strike immediate interest unless you are a candidate for an executive position which just happens to be open. It never hurts to be aligned with the ideals and goals represented by the organization you will work for. Nonprofits are not typically as materially gratifying and you will experience boundless frustration if you expect lot's of praise.

Naturally there are many types of companies left unmentioned. There are government contractors, mid-sized private and public companies, joint-ventures and a host of others. I glossed a few typical structures and provided cursory discussion to get you thinking. Common to each approach is the idea that you choose a target, understand what is important to them, research, present your background to the right people accordingly and in the right way and by default you will have set yourself apart from most. Ultimately I will encourage you to take it further by defining and creating your own job. Technique and application details are provided over the course of this book.

The last discussion for this chapter is to derail the traditional approaches to finding work – quite simply they were long-shots during the prosperous 1990s and for now erase any idea they existed. To do so I need to dig them up for you.

Let's start by discussing the role of a part of any organization you should bypass the best you can. Human Resource Departments – generally speaking HR Departments serve employment law compliance and very seldom serve the function of getting anyone a job. True, they post positions, staff trade fairs, run ads, pre-screen applicants, write the company policy manual, negotiate insurance rates, and schedule sexual harassment training but they do not define the needs of an organization. Sending your resume to an HR Department is peeing up the proverbial rope. The single exception is if your goal is work in HR and the HR Manager has an opening. Then, technically, you are contacting an HR Department. In this example the HR Manager is the hiring manager - the person who knows if there is an actual organizational need and is directly responsible for filling the position. Apart from that sending material to an HR department without the guiding hand of a hiring manager from another department will essentially never lead to an interview – consider dealing with HR an essential evil.

Answering wanted ads in trade journals and newspapers. Unless you are seeking an entry-level clerk or an executive-level position forget it. Professional openings are almost never sincerely addressed this way. Many positions are publically posted, but again, that annoying legal topic requires posting an ad and giving the public their perceived fair swing. Occasionally a trade journal will sincerely post an executive level position that is tough to fill. Usually a head-hunter posted the ad.

Job fairs. This might have merit if you have a specific hand-in-glove fit for an opening. I do think this approach is valid for certain engineering disciplines, health-care, finance, and soon-to-be-graduated college students. This is under the "can't hurt department" but seldom do I invest much faith in this approach. Generally speaking this is almost an activity that should be avoided. For the mid-level professional it's largely a waste of time. The delusion that you will have a face-to-face opportunity should be dispelled by consideration that it's usually an HR representative who will dutifully shake your hand and place your resume in a large pile never to remember you nor possess the ability to meaningfully recommend you for hire.

Answering on-line postings - remember the era we are now in? The odds of you differentiating yourself by joining the masses is de facto insanity. On-line options have been available long enough to become tradition. Skip it. Given its ease you will join untold numbers. Legitimate on-line venues are normally sent as assigned links via a would-be hiring manager. These are sent to specific individuals only. These are not broadly distributed. General public postings are usually an EEOC compliance measure.

Posting on Monster.com or similar…other than to alert your present employer (if you have one) hiring managers and head-hunters rarely run keyword searches to see if you're out there. Again, this won't necessarily do you any harm but please don't expect results either.

Drop from your vernacular the expression "job search". This implies a litany of jobs that you will thumb through in search of the opportunity that most closely resembles what you are looking for or something that puts food on the table for now. The emphasis in this book is to help guide you toward creating opportunity where today there may not be one. It's a novel approach to most. Successful folks have employed it in their careers. It takes more time, more research, and a focused approach. I am not saying there isn't merit in listening to, for example, what head-hunters have to offer. You should certainly be a "known commodity". Ultimately, though, some of the best positions were never borne in the traditional way.

At the end of this book you should have the framework to identify what you want to do and how to sell yourself into either an advertised position or more ideally, create a position. Let's visit that comment again…yes, I said create a position. With the right approach you have the ability to convince a company they need your services badly enough to create a position for you. We live in a new time. Unemployment for some will last years. Perhaps one day we can restore fiscal discipline to a limited government and enjoy the byproduct of a system that supports a free market but you may need work now! I also share my thoughts on what you need to do to remain in demand, establish a good network in the event you lose your job or wish to move to something better, and put yourself in a good position to make moves internally. You do not want to leave your career path up to the whims of your boss, larger organizational directives, or chance. Moving yourself onward and upward is an endless pursuit…your success depends on more than chance.

Chapter Two – What Are You Chasing?

So, let's hone in on you. What's your situation? Are you working? If you do not have a job you may be desperate to find anything without regard to eventual career direction. If you have a job that you hate and want to do something else then at least you have an income while looking and you can take more time. You may be one of the lucky few these days who actually likes your job but sense that now is a good time to consider another path either internally or working for a new company.

Potential motivations for finding a new job are widely varied. However, approaches to defining and finding work are worthy of a focused method – one that will likely land you in a better spot not too terribly far in the future.

Back to you. My advice to you if you are not working is simply to do whatever you can to get income going. You can work on the finesse portion later. Do not make the mistake of not working until you find "a good fit". If you are able to land something deemed worthy quickly then great! If not, be willing to do something else in the interim – long periods of unemployment do not help and your willingness to do whatever is needed to create income shows well in any interview. Do virtually anything to capture income while you are "looking". The economic doldrums as of this writing are two years old and will likely last another ten. There is no shame in "settling" for something – especially if you don't look at it as permanent.

Now to the more complex – maybe you are working in a field commensurate with your background but you are not happy. You must think through things clearly. So, why do you hate your job? Your boss? You feel there is no upward potential? Tired of "same-ol'-shit-new-day"? It will help if you can identify the source of malcontent. At some point in our careers all of us imagine things to be much better somewhere else. I'm not sure where this originates. It may be part of some genetic code that compels us to explore – exploration in your career is not bad per se but you want to bring cool reason to bear in career matters. Any job contains unsavory aspects. Constant customer complaints, a micromanaging supervisor, bureaucratic organization structure, endless trainings and meetings, working you to the bone because of the "do-more-with-less" approach, any of these can lead you to believe it's better somewhere else. Be careful.

There certainly are good reasons to search outside of your company but I'll arm you with a few thoughts. It normally takes you two years to recover financially from a change in careers even if your pay shows a nominal increase. Consider this if you are in the mid or upper management ranks. When you leave a job you forsake bonus that you might have earned had you stayed (many positions at this level have some type of stock options or bonus that matures later). When you join a new company similar bonuses do not kick in for a while. If your new position requires relocation you will suffer setbacks even in a company-paid move. Your 401K and Fidelity accounts if you have them are not trivial. You will interrupt their growth by leaving.

When you decide it's time to move make certain you know why and really investigate whether or not you can pursue new opportunity within the company you work for. More often than not this is a better alternative. You will not necessarily be happier under a different banner. All jobs have their pitfalls.

O.k. you may fall into another category where you were and still are happy in your role but you feel it's time to move up. Great! I couldn't be happier for you. Again, work to identify why you feel it's time and what you will do for your company in a new role that will add benefit to the company. In this case it's even better if your manager agrees.

I have some general advice when it comes to changing jobs and preparing to take on something new. You've heard the adage that you need to "run to something" and not "run from something". Especially in the current economic climate you do not want to be sabotaged by typical self-destructive thinking. Careers bring with them disappointment and pain by definition. You won't find remedy running to something else. In my experience working for four major corporations, a small private company, and doing contract work for a litany of others, no place offers Nirvana. All jobs provide a cross for you to bear if you view it so.

I am not trying to dissuade you from chasing something new - absolutely not the case. After all, this is a book on how to identify opportunity and get work. I am simply asking you to reflect and be clinical. Until you've exhausted all internal options you may be hurting yourself in the long run by doing something spontaneous. Many people leave to find out they were not far away from a promotion or had they stayed, other opportunities would have been theirs. Once you leave, a door may have closed for good.

Why do you work? Skip the temptation to wax philosophical. Most of us chose an education and training that we thought would lead to a good income. Without exploring what we'd really like to do we followed roughly the same path of building credentials, finding related work, starting a family, and then pondering whether or not we were fulfilled. Unless you are in the clergy, internal medicine, or leading a non-profit, there are few venues with a true calling. The trick, like a marriage, is to work hard to be the best in what might otherwise be a mundane pursuit. The best performer in anything is well compensated and fulfilled from a standpoint of accomplishment. It matters much less what you do but how you do it. If, in fact, you are working for people who truly retard your potential or you believe you need to pursue something else, then by all means look to other companies and organizations for your fit – be aware, though, the potential cost in change.

So, here is why I am spending so much time with introspection. The path that I will present showing you how to pursue a career is built on the idea that you know what you want to do and more specifically how you intend to help a company. Even if you are not clear on your "chosen" pursuit, you will want at least describe your stated direction and do it well. One of my choice lessons is that it is not important that you are spiritually fulfilled by your chosen work. What is important is that you perform as advertised.

Let me talk for a minute about the traditional process of finding work. Most of us are sucked into the idea that an employer has a clear picture on what their needs are, who can best fill it, and a prospective employer has all the cards. Like lemmings we answer want ads, respond to headhunter calls, attend trade fairs, talk to human resource representatives from other firms in hopes that our great opportunity rests in someone else's hands. Now, certainly you can find a job in the traditional way, though the odds are on par with winning the lottery as of this writing. I will teach you methods that will vastly tip the odds in your favor whether you pursue traditional paths to finding work or you create opportunity. Defining what you are looking for is a critical first step because it allows you to choose opportunities that will work for you and more importantly allow you to define how you will benefit someone else.

If you are looking for new opportunity, rather than search blindly, try writing down what it is that you are looking for. Difficult? Probably. Try something easier to get you started. What don't you like about your current situation? That should be easy. Write it down! Now, consider the remedy to your discontent. What would that be? My guess it roughly the opposite to that trait that you don't like. Write it down. If you hate the bureaucracy at your job than you would be motivated by a streamlined business structure – write it down. Do not move on to the next chapter unless you can list five attributes of a job you would like to have. My guess is those five attributes will speak less to the functional aspects of a job than the environment you work in. Get that on paper. This is your first assignment.

O.k. that wasn't as easy as you thought it would be (most likely). Maybe you are one of the rare few who knew exactly what you wanted to do. Most only know they are unhappy. Here's my next assignment. Are you able to address the five attributes you are looking for that could be fulfilled either in your current role or at another role in the company you now work for? If so document where and how. If not, then before you start the random-walk of job searching, it will help if you can identify a situation where you would be able to address your desires.

Let's assume that now you are clear in why you want to pursue a particular job. Are you good at sales? Specifically are you good at selling you? Do you know what that means? It's time to learn if you don't already know. That's essentially what the rest of this book is about along with a few detours. I will try to help give you tools to better sell yourself – doesn't that sound funny? Get used to the idea. It's fascinating to consider how poorly established professionals prepare themselves for the job search – there may be an intrinsic assumption that experience is its own merit. Such professionals are often great at what they do. They just have a hell of a time explaining the good they will provide to a prospect. In the "new economy" you will simply have to do a good job promoting yourself and researching opportunity if you are going to have an enjoyable career. It won't be easy. Much will be asked of you. As I detail in the chapters to follow your career search will be unending. Doing the things that place you at an advantage will always be in play.

During the 1990s and early 2000s getting a job was easy for anyone with a good background. In a sense we didn't have to engage in much pre-planning discipline. Careers just sort of happened. You chased open postings or replied to a head hunter and the odds were in your favor – something would result. In a sense not having to put forth effort beyond replying to ads and interviewing was a disservice to all. There wasn't the need to identify a best fit in a job opportunity and build a plan on how you would help a prospective employer. You didn't have to show up with a plan. Welcome to a post 2010 world. The traditional approaches will no longer work. You need new methods. Learn them now and you will have a head start on your competition.

A few thoughts to leave you with:

- ❖ If you've put in at least ten years into a specific career, there is a cost to switch paths. Most people grossly underestimate how much this will hurt you financially. Don't switch careers wholesale unless you've weighed your options.
- ❖ To paraphrase unless you get at least a twenty-percent boost in compensation by switching companies, my best advice is not to. Try to be clinical as opposed to reactive and see if you can find a situation or morph your current job to address your discontent.
- ❖ Please follow my suggestion and carefully document what you are looking for. You need to be very clear in what you might want to pursue rather than why you want to leave.
- ❖ Again, if you do not have a job, don't hold out for something that matches past pay. You need income now and you will want to minimize "empty-time" on your resume.
- ❖ No problem in searching for a new career if you already have one – most of us do. Be aware, though that there will never be a perfect role with zero agony.
- ❖ You will want to take a different path from the "masses" if your goal is to find new employment.
- ❖ As I point out later in the book age discrimination is not as rampant as some would have you believe – that's great news! What you need to be aware of, however, mid-life is not a time for career soul searching. You need to be "firing on all cylinders" relative to what you do well. This doesn't mean you can't do what you do for a new employer, but starting a new career from scratch (unless you're already wealthy) probably isn't wise.
- ❖ Profit is good. It is a measure of an organization's viability. Sorry to defend the obvious but these are weird times – we need to counter the assault on free-enterprise.

❖ Get used to the idea of selling your capabilities. Prospective employers really don't carry the burden of figuring out how you will help them. You must tell the story.

❖ We live in a new age. The economy will likely get worse…not better. It is critical that you learn new skills in creating opportunity for yourself.

Chapter Three – Preparatory Concepts

Be known and know others. I want to share what this has meant to me and how I've used it. Most people give casual reference to the term and the meanings are assumed. It merits more discussion because this is the essence of how you will avail yourself opportunity. I am assuming you "do good work" and are well thought of. If not, anonymity may improve your odds. Being known works both ways. The obvious part of networking means that you will exchange contact information with people you meet professionally. You will know what they do and how you might benefit one another. You will want to meet as many people as you can internally, suppliers, and customers. That covers the nauseatingly obvious stuff.

Now the meat. A database with several hundred contacts may be somewhat useful. Here's a concept, build friendships with people you like who work in fields you would like to be in or people who call on professions you might like to work in. Whorish? Look, people tend to compartmentalize between social and professional worlds. In Europe and Latin America merging the two is one business lesson Americans can learn from. Obviously find people you like but more to the point, seek people who are connected somehow to fields you would like to be in. Get beyond the superficial. If "only" a friendship results then you've captured the best part. Have a need and who will pull for you? Someone you were introduced to briefly or your friend? The term "networking" is cliché but I cannot offer a better alternative. There is a variant in how I use it, though. Your goal should never be to swap cards with as many people as you can and maintain a massive Rolodex in case you need to call someone up. The high-quality low-volume approach is more important. You will want to build better than superficial relationships with people occupying influential roles rather than taking the shotgun approach.

After ten years of getting to know people in a social context who might also serve as a professional contact there are probably not two people between you and someone making hiring decisions in your target field. Those you know likely know someone directly who can hire you or they "know someone who knows someone." There is an old adage that you are no more than seven people away from anyone in the world. I'll skip the mathematics but take from it the elementary concept that for each added friend you have your opportunities are exponentially enhanced.

O.k. so what if I'm an introvert? Say a stereotypical IT type who would is more comfortable with code than people? You cannot change who you are but step out and challenge yourself. Find people. Cultivate friendships. If you're truly an introvert than I'm sorry, accept the fact you won't have as much opportunity to branch out. I don't think most people really wish to live in social isolation. Business, as it is, is really about people. Something I had to learn early in my career. In school I thought my engineering prowess would be its own merit. My first post-graduate career was in sales. The lessons learned and the associations made in those first few years breathed opportunity and choices.

Almost to a fault consistently stay in touch with your professionally connected friends. People have a way of dropping communication as they move or change jobs. Friendships I made a decade or more ago now living in other parts of the country have been the ones to help put me in touch with new opportunities. Conventional but fantastic advice - join trade associations or participate in chambers of commerce. You will meet people who can help you. And here's another snippet of wisdom. Never be ashamed to ask what you are looking for. Tell people. Assuming you can maneuver in such a manner as not to imperil your current job.

Most of the stories I can offer illustrating how others employed contacts to help get hired involve asking for help from people they knew well. That's most often the case and has the best chance of providing you with concrete help. There are exceptions and I would encourage you to engage in dialogue even with people you don't know well. Sometimes you will be surprised and a relative stranger can help. I offer this as a personal testimony. My wife had been a mechanical engineer working only two years after graduating from a university in her home country before leaving for the United States in 1993. We married in 1994. In 2008 we moved to the Huntsville, AL area as I changed careers (more on that later) to work for a well-known steel company having a mill in the area. Huntsville, AL is primarily an aerospace and Department of Defense (DOD) hub. At the time we moved she was still of the opinion that she never really wanted to work outside the home. Things changed. By 2010 the steel business hurting and my bonus potential diminished, the kids were now teenagers and my wife began to feel as if former talents, now atrophied, were forever gone. This epiphany led to her launching a job search in the beginning of that year. Naturally we talked to neighbors, friends, associates and work, and she went to trade shows, job-fairs, wherever she could talk to representatives from potential employers. The economy had already stalled. Under the Obama Administration NASA, the aerospace industry in general, and DOD were just about the only facets of the government slated for cuts. Times were bad locally and nationally.

My wife's prospects were poor at best. She was educated in mechanical engineering in a foreign university, had not worked for seventeen years, and was quickly approaching forty-two years of age. All of this coupled with a failing economy should have dissuaded her from trying. She was active and did many things. Backing up to 2009 she enrolled in a series of ProEngineer 3-D CAD courses to help update her skills. She recruited references (personal) and began networking in earnest. We met many people who at least placed her resume in front of people who were looking. We continually ran into the hurdle of her needing very specific experience. Too often we were met with this sincere sentiment, "If only you were here four years ago when things were hot – you would have ten job offers within a week. I am sorry but we are cutting staff and only hiring very specifically trained people when we do hire." It was easy to get discouraged.

Chapter 3

In April of 2010 I joined delegations from two local chambers of commerce on a Washington D.C. trip. During a social hour I met maybe twenty people – mostly just circulated. Politics won the bulk of any conversation as both the steel industry and the aerospace/DOD contingent sought to bolster their position with Alabama Congressmen and Senators. At some point I met with a handful of men from the DOD world. I introduced myself as the only "non-DOD" person living on my street. I struck up a short conversation with a gentleman who seemed interested to hear how the steel business was being affected by the Administration. We covered that for a while and then the conversation faded. He had mentioned his involvement with one of the larger aerospace companies in the area. While turning to walk away it struck me that I may have missed an opportunity to bring up my wife. I did a 180, came back to the man and told him that on a personal note my wife was looking to begin her career in the U.S. I went into enough detail regarding her background that by chance a key point of interest was piqued. It turns out the gentleman was a well-positioned in the company and possessed both the understanding of how my wife might help but also wielded influence. He was quite aware of the company's involvement with the same overseas organization my wife had worked for. Her fluency now in both languages coupled with her background placed her on a very short list of people who could help under direct employ. He offered his card and asked to have her call. My wife now works for that company! She secured work in her field at the same time others were being let go. All odds were stacked against her…at least from a conventional approach. It is easy to dismiss this chance encounter as blind luck. Albeit we count our blessings in the good fortune of that meeting it pays to remember that we had already spoken with scores of people and would continue to do so until we found an opportunity.

Now the subtext to this story is far more complex. I will give you that. My wife still needed a very specific skill-set, the demand had to be there, and the presentation of her background had to be quite good. She sold her story well and both sides understood the value that she could bring. Consider this, though – had her story not reached the right person she likely would not have gotten a shot. Her skills were unique. A company actually could benefit greatly from what she had to offer. Yet, not a soul in an H.R. department or anyone in a front-line role would likely have a clue how she might be able to help. In better times perhaps she would have been hired in another capacity and worked her way toward this role but time would have been wasted in the process. It took four more months to interview, sell her story, engage in persistent dialogue with department heads in the company, but without the initial introduction there never would have been a meaningful connection between the company and what my wife offered.

Focusing this discussion on you is simple. You must learn to prospect and do it well. Reach out to people. Co-workers, friends, people from industry circles, people you meet from professional trade organizations, neighbors, anyone. Prospecting is likely the most important sales tool in gaining you career opportunity. It's got to be ongoing throughout your career. Even if you feel you never want to change jobs within or to another organization you will need access to the people who can help. They're not listed in the yellow pages and the front desk isn't going to forward your call.

You never need to be a "glad-hander", obnoxious, intrusive, or a pain-in-the-ass. Just a smile and a brief introduction – should friendship follow, all the better. Cultivate relationships and stay in touch.

Becoming well-connected takes time. To revive the tired analogy of planting seeds is actually appropriate. Where my wife's situation started from scratch, at any time there are three or four major companies I could work for tomorrow by calling a current friend working in an influential role. They know what I did for them, they know what I'm capable of, and they occasionally ask if I'm happy in my current job. These are relationships that in some cases are closing in on twenty years in length! You nurture these relationships as they become the most valuable thing you will ever have.

Think about your situation, you know suppliers, customers, co-workers and people outside of your work environment who may be connected to fields you'd like to be in. Even if you are comfortable at this time you cannot count on when you will need the help of others. It's much easier to grow friendship when there is no direct need. Should a time come when you wish to use the help of friends things go much more smoothly if you are calling on someone you know for help.

The simple pieces to staying connected are worth discussing. Maintain address lists, drop an email now and then, better yet call and say hello. Check in and see how things are going. To a fault people in your life disappear when they don't need something. Switch roles for a minute. How would it make you feel if someone you barely knew called you only to ask for a reference favor or two speak a few words of support since he was trying to get hired at your company? How much effort would you go to? If a trusted friend were to call and ask the same favors your effort would be sincere - very basic.

One more aspect of cultivating friends who can help; it's strange but few people have learned to ask favors. Perhaps most people err in trying to be polite. Ask yourself this, have you ever felt offended if a friend calls and wants to know about an opening in your company or wants advice on how best to approach a Vice President of Operations regarding how they can help? This life is short. You need to ask for what you want. It is impossible to know all the key people who can help you and aspects of the business you are shielded from but there are people who can lead you to those answers. The benefit of networking cannot be overstated.

Being known is crucial. Building friendships instead of fleeting acquaintance is even more important. Having something of value that you can offer those you know is the second part of the story.

Avoiding the entitlement trap – always go beyond in your job.
Being connected opens lines of communication. If you stink at

what you do, this will be revealed. I hope the reverse holds in your case. Being connected helps if people have good things to say about you. After twenty-four years working in varied career paths I have grown to understand a few attributes of the collective human psyche. Number one is the insistence by nearly all of us that we deserve more than what we're paid. As such few push beyond the HR expectations in their role. It's almost as if you lose out in some kind of deal by giving more than what you are expected to do. You would be well served to bring far more value to your employer than what your pay would suggest rather than resenting the notion. "Pay me first, and then I'll do it!" That type of thinking is both dangerous and stupid.

What's fascinating about this common self-deception is that it blinds you to the reality extra effort will eventually bring returns to you far outweighing the pro-rated increase in pay. And I'm not discussing monumental extra work. Since the landscape in this regard is nearly level, you don't have to push too hard to stand out. As coworkers fall into the pattern of swapping weekend stories on Monday, "winding down" and cutting out early on Friday, and fulfilling work requirements only as they arise, it's easy for anyone to excel in a relative way.

At a minimum do these things:

1) Write down what you influence in your work.

2) Write down at least three goals you would like to see met within "your sphere of influence" in the next six months.

3) Meet those goals – execution is key.

4) Write down what goals you would like your department to achieve in the next year outside of "your sphere of influence." Work with others to table these goals and help the group drive them if they are adopted.

5) As you begin to pursue your goals under item 2), let your boss know what you are working on. Get his or her buy-in and then as you complete the items, report the progress. If telling the boss makes you feel like you're kissing butt, skip it. But document what you did, what you learned, and the impact to your department.

6) Remember, only you really give-a-shit how your kids did in sports, school, etc. As your co-workers self-validate by swapping kid stories you need to minimize your participation and get to work. Obviously be polite, smile, tell the occasional illustrative anecdote, but for God's Sake! Abandon the hours down the drain each week to solve the country's political issues, discuss unfair treatment of so-and-so, and all the usual water-cooler crap that consumes the year.

7) Try putting in a half an hour more work each day. If you're in the legal or medical professions this does not apply since work is all that you do. For many of us in "corporate world" we tell other people we put in sixty hours when forty is the norm. This isn't for consumption…the idea is not brownie points. The idea is that you are actually going to deliver more value to your employer. Try spending a quiet fifteen minutes before others arrive to plan out your day.

8) Plan your day. Your quintessential corporate type shows up with a vague recollection of what meetings are happening today but the ball game is still fresh on the brain and he or she will deal with events as they happen. If there is idle time there's lots of politics to chat about and plenty of willing audiences. Actually writing down your daily goals and following through is an amazing thing!

9) Document the value you bring. If you don't understand the value you bring to your employer there is a good chance you bring very little. Deal with facts at review time. This helps. The hours and days you put in matter only in what you are able to accomplish. It's what you get done – duh! This will also aid what you can tell other people you've done. Most people struggle to write a resume…it's difficult to articulate what you haven't thought about.

10) Make it a point to learn what others are doing outside of your department. If you do make time to socialize at work, try instead visiting with department heads outside your area and learn the business! Ask them about their priorities. You learn and they consider you interested.

11) Unless you work for a secretive private company try drafting the Profit-and-Loss statement for your division and for the corporation. Understand where the profit comes from and related challenges. Even if you are a warehouse forklift driver! I don't care! Understand your company's business. In this way you may be able to quantify how your efforts affect your company's profitability.

Are you doing these things now? If not, start. If so, congratulations! Even if you are considered a mediocre lackey one year of doing the above will cause opinions to change. Trust me! Falling into the trap of feeling you deserve more is to be blind to your overseas competition (which by the way is already putting downward pressure on U.S. salaries). When unemployment exceeds 15% you will see people's attitudes change. Until then, you are presented with an unbelievable opportunity to differentiate yourself in the best way.

It should be clear why being the best at what you do enhances your marketability inside and outside of your company. It also creates demand for you. No one that matters is in touch with your intentions and self-perception. All anyone will really care about is what you can do for them. Make sure it's significant!

Live within your means. What has this trite statement have to do with finding a job or getting a better one? Buying a book on how to improve your odds in the interview process and progress in your career didn't entail financial planning advice did it? I'll make this a short discussion.

Financial desperation puts you in a horrible frame-of-mind for negotiations. Also, owing money feeds the insanity discussed in the previous section. The angst from working hard and owing money typically leads to the idea you are not paid what you are worth even though it is you who simply cannot balance the finances.

Where "success breeds success" when you are negotiating for an opportunity and it is clear that you will be fine with or without it your odds are vastly improved. Obviously we work for money and opportunity. The misuse of money, though, is akin to a crack-addict wild-eyed and desperate to move up in the world if only to fuel an uncontrolled addiction to having stuff. This presents a backward dynamic. You don't get the job because you need the money – you get the job because an organization needs the value you bring…the money follows. If you are the type of person finding that they often owe money and cannot stay ahead it's usually more a matter of money management than how much you earn. Earning more will likely not solve your problems. Your spending will simply climb in response to a higher income.

I'm addressing a problem afflicting most people today - if not you then possibly your significant other. Having lived the misery I can tell you how to avoid it. It's simple. Create a spreadsheet capturing your monthly expenses and income is where you start – my rule of thumb is that your income must exceed your expenses (and I mean everything) by at least 10% - period. Until the income side changes you must deal with the expense side. This relates to the entitlement thinking as well. You don't need new cars, multiple cell phones (kids certainly don't "need" them), cable TV, I-Pods, etc. It's usually those monthly drains that will take you down. When you clinically list each expense then you must make choices. You can then see where you need to trim. Finances are usually highly emotionally charged. Here's the advice where I'll get sued. Regarding marriage, if either partner simply cannot come to terms with this method of thinking your relationship is doomed! I don't care how much you think you are in love, if one is a consummate debtor you cannot make it. If both are consummate debtors you probably deserve one another but if one is intent on doing the right thing and the other won't then the right thing is a divorce! As expensive as that is you need to cut your losses and you stand a chance of recouping. This is serious stuff folks. We are a nation of debtors. Something has gone terribly awry. Once we're off to work we cannot wait for all of the good stuff to follow. There is little discipline. We're told this drives an economy. I beg to differ. A nation cannot spend its way to prosperity. The evidence in the U.S. mounts every day.

Quite the philosophical departure from the intent of this book, huh? Not at all. Distractions in your personal life may sabotage your effectiveness at work drain energy needed to focus on doing well. Try interviewing for a new career when the overwhelming goal is simply more pay and you will have trouble communicating why you are the person who will benefit the position the most. Not insignificant is the fairly new practice of companies running a credit report on their candidates. Imagine being qualified for a job in every way but failing because your credit score sucks. Other than finance positions I generally think the candidate credit check borders on infringement of your privacy but it's a growing practice. It is reality. My final word is somewhat spiritual. Call it Karma, or what have you, but when you are successful and happy good things seem to be easy to come by. Your contentment shows through in all things. Interviews not excluded.

Add to your credentials. All right, so I've covered knowing the right people, doing well in your job, and advising you not to be stupid with your money. Now I am introducing an obvious and basic topic that I must cover because so few invest a little extra time to give themselves this important advantage. Purchasing, accounting, engineering, human resources, EH&S, research-and-development,…,whatever your field there are professional credentials that will enhance your marketability. Oh, sales - can't forget you! In this case there are industry-specific credentials and/or associations that may help your cause. Take part! This goes for anyone.

Almost without exception your employer will pay the bill for you to get added schooling, training, testing, and whatever else is required to obtain said credentials. Take advantage of this while employed! If there are re-up charges to stay current with any licensure this is normally covered as well. A current CPA license for accounting, an SPHR certificate for human resources, or a PE license for engineering are examples of certification that will help set you apart. Not an end-all but essential for certain positions and at a minimum something that sets you apart. What this offers at the very least is added credibility. Do it! Watch less TV for a year and get this out of the way.

Trade an idle hour in your day for something useful. Alright, now I've gone too far! You just wanted to learn how to interview effectively and I'm telling you how to run your life! What the hell is this crap? Sorry. I can't resist giving you life advice that will help stack the odds in your favor for many things – an interview included. Have you heard the adage "sympathy can be found in the dictionary…it's between 'shit' and 'syphilis'"? That's about how I feel when people whine about not having enough time. Bullshit! You fill at least a few hours of the day ineffectively. You still can! I'm only asking you to think of a self-development pursuit to supplant T.V., bickering with your spouse, idle stuff at work, basically any passive activity you pursue out of boredom. You want better results? Put in at least incremental added effort and you may get there.

Here are a few ideas in no order of importance:

1 – Public speaking via Toastmasters or another similar venue. Many, especially in technical or financial venues don't often get the chance at work and don't pride themselves with this ability. People do in fact judge your ability to present. Seldom is this a natural skill. Most often it's learned. Learn. You really have to be better-than-average to be listened to. Most people clap when the mundane close their speech – they are usually celebrating the termination. Enough cannot be said about your ability to communicate verbally in front of a group. An office drone with presentation talent has upward mobility. A talented worker with awful presentation skills has little opportunity. Put aside resistance, fear, and all the other excuses and go after this one.

2 - Learn a language. May take you five plus years at an hour a day but business in Latin America and China will likely provide more opportunity going forward than the U.S.

3 – Read trade journals related to your field.

4 – Study politics. The notion of the U.S. remaining a representative republic is under siege as in no time prior. A working knowledge of our Constitution should give you an appreciating how far we've departed. Your resulting acumen will likely make for interesting conversation – remember that people stuff?

5 – Work out. Fat folks are less likely to be hired than fit folks. More on prejudice later.

6 – Take a class. Again, your company will likely pay you for it and you can bolster your worth.

Investing just a little time into a single talent each week will give you proficiency in a few years. This may be an item that sways a decision, differentiates you against those who waste their free-time, provides an edge that allows your to more successfully perform a job, and at the very least improves you!

I want you to consider something. You've heard much about the "global economy". You may be enveloped by it and understand it. There is an aspect about our interconnectedness with Asia Pacific, Latin America, The EU, etc. that you probably understand yet avoid thinking about (it's hard to come to terms with facts that are unpleasant or threatening). Understanding how companies compete globally it easy to see. Taking it further now that companies are, to an extent, borderless, so is there ability to obtain talent. Is it a little unsettling to think that you may be competing with someone who makes a fifth what you do and their skills are honed razor sharp courtesy of the fact they grew up in squalor and had both the motivation and few distractions of idle time. Free markets do compensate for iniquity. Your talent had better be up to snuff from now on. Americans as a group are fat and ready for slaughter. There is less that differentiates our ingenuity, work-ethic, and resources from others today as in the past. Have you visited South Korea lately? China? India? You can no longer hide behind being American. What used to make us unique has largely been eroded by runaway politics. We have become a nation of entitlement - seeking an ever-growing Federal Government to solve what we once solved for ourselves.

Make a clear self-assessment of who you are. While much of this nation is rooted in denial you can position yourself favorably by facing what is real and turning off the TV for a while. Be disciplined with your time. I'm not asking you to forsake all that you enjoy. But note this. Should you "only" work, spend a moment here and there with the family, watch TV, mess around in the yard, etc. you can look at your life and identify a small slice of time during the day that if invested differently would ensure you continued to be viable for employment at least and potentially accelerate your career at best. Should you choose to do nothing your days are numbered insofar as commanding professional level rewards. You need to give yourself every advantage.

Learn to sell yourself. Sound cheap and tawdry? Ignore the connotation and get going - you must learn. In upcoming chapters I detail how but get ready. You have to be your best promoter. Somewhere in our youth we are taught to be humble. In a sense that is good but at the same time most people cannot stand the thought of promoting themselves. It seems so vain, so self-absorbed. It's not. To succeed in anything you need to market your idea. In this case it is you! No one can be as effective as you. Accept that you must learn and read on!

Chapter Four – Presentation & Interview Scenarios

Prejudice, pre-judging - human resource departments and lawyers write volumes on why this is bad. We all do it and will forever more. Age, sex, race, apparent sexual orientation, height, weight, voice, mannerisms…hundreds of overt attributes assimilate in the mind of an audience creating a picture of you.

So much fuss over qualifications. Aside from neurosurgery and C++ programming very few positions demand hand-in-glove perfect-fit qualifications. Job descriptions may suggest this but that's not even close. Think about it. If you were interviewing, would you rather hire someone who could learn relatively quickly and is likeable or someone who obviously "has issues" and could work the functional aspects of a job flawlessly?

I'm going to assume that you are smart enough to understand the basics regarding appearance and presentation. In our do-more-with-less approach to business, time is fleeting and judging candidates or opportunities is often superficial. It's critical that you do not undermine your value and your chances by making a poor impression. On that note here's as close to the self-help approach as I'll get:

1) Your body - not much you can do about your genes but if you are significantly overweight you will be judged as a liability…even by the fat! Are you fat? Step aside weight-loss programs, here's mine. Cut your caloric intake immediately by 500 calories per day and work out almost strenuously ('till you break a sweat) for twenty to thirty minutes each day beginning right now! Oh, My God! I can hear the back-lash! "You are not a medical doctor and you have no idea what I am living through!" My retort? Sue me if you wish. The obesity in the mirror is a result of too much food and too little burn. Jettison the excuses you've been given as to why you're unique! Switch the intake calorie to burn ratio and you will lose weight! Aside from the benefits to your health and life overall you will no

longer be judged as a slob once your body approaches "normality". You can begin today without a workout machine or weights. Try this…pushups (start with a handful) followed by jumping up and down on two legs until you are at least breathing hard, followed by sit-ups (start with just a few), followed by high-kicks (try kicking your hands placing them straight out in front of your body – try five each leg). After doing one set of each until you are breathing rapidly, regain your breath and repeat twice for a total of three "circuits". Increase the number of each exercise you do as the weeks progress. As you lose weight and gain strength you might consider alternative and more stressful workouts. Weight lost in this manner will be closer to permanent since fat will be shed and muscle will grow…the latter burns calories. So many side-benefits to getting your weight down. And by the way, to sound blasphemous, it's not that fucking hard! Stop making excuses. No one gives a shit why you're fat. Do what I have told you and you will see sustained weight loss beginning in the first few weeks and accelerating as you increase your activity.

Are you too skinny? Now there's one you don't hear too often! After checking for tape-worm try upping your caloric intake by 400 calories per day and engage in resistance training. If you have an eating disorder please put down this book and check into a recovery program, your issues are deeper than I can address. Unless your ribs are visible and you are gaunt, there aren't as many social stigmas for being skinny but you want to project a vision of health (or at least not detract from the notion).

If you are physically disabled none of the body-type discriminatory discussions really apply. You will have your own unique challenges in convincing people you are apt and able. Likely your courage for showing up at an interview will be considered but with any luck you are chasing a cerebral pursuit and not firefighting.

That about covers the discussion on how your body may influence an interview…except sexuality. I didn't cover this but it is important. Again, in a contemporary manner we are trained that this does not exist. PR crap! If you are female and attractive you have an upper-hand in swaying the male side of the world but you might equally piss off your gender in the interview process. Completely covering up your sexual prowess is equally bad as displaying too much. This is a tight-rope but if played well it will open doors like no force in the universe. Select your clothes to at least suggest your form without overplaying. I recall interviewing candidates with tits propped up and out for nearly full view. What the candidate may have considered enticing looked completely stupid in context. What works at 2:00 am in a bar doesn't fly in business. By contrast I've participated in panel interviews where a pleasant looking woman selected professional dress that did not entirely hide her attributes. The female interviewers may have been mildly irritated but the candidate's qualifications were not lost in her presentation. The men were…well, men. Sick bastards that they are they appreciated her appearance but also were able to see beyond the candidate's form. As a note of interest the hire was made and this young lady is doing extremely well in her career a decade later.

Male sexual prowess? Not much to comment on here. If you are good-looking and energetic your chances are enhanced. Regarding clothing, men don't have to wear push-up bras and blouses at most interviews so there is nothing to say other than don't go too cheap on the suit! No grandpa suits with the belt-loops under your armpits. Obvious stuff.

2) Your speech – how you form words, sentences, and ideas may be clear and concise. It needs to be! This is harder to self-judge. You may want to get feedback from a trusted friend. Do you ramble? Do you form your thoughts while your mouth is open or while talking? How is your voice? Too quiet? Too loud? Ideally you are pleasant, to the point, and have about the right volume. For business purposes stray from quaint anecdotes initially. These may have value later when you know the audience but be open and willing to share information without putting yourself into a "category" as perceived by the listener.

3) Your humility – have some – unless you are running for Congress.

4) Non business subject matter – clearly you are not simply a work robot. Whether you are interviewing for a job or selling your services people want to work with someone they like and can relate to. Allow the interviewer to open up discussion on you. Again, the obvious. Under no circumstances delve into religion or politics. Stray from anything that might stop anyone from smiling. Keep in light, superficial, and for the Love of God, avoid topics that provide too much detail. Turn it around a bit too if you'd like. Ask the interviewers what they do for fun. After you've worked with someone for twenty years they can learn about your phobias, biases, food allergies, divorce, and so on. Reveal little but don't dodge the questions.

5) How do you engage people? Are you bossy? Shy? Laid-back? Overzealous? In-your-face? Awkward? Find that feedback friend of yours again and have a discussion. It may be difficult for you to self-evaluate how you come across. Study approaches you like. Emulate. Aggression-as-a-virtue in business is oversold. Don't. Polite, respectful, informative when asked, assertive when called for is a nice blend in any venue.

6) Your writing skills. Those little "forks-in-the-road" that
lead to your life's destination. When your straight path
reaches a branch…one opportunity versus the other. A
popular view is that you will have to decide which way you
will go. Sometimes your own limitations will send you in
one direction instead – maybe not the direction you'd
hoped for.

Imagine two people with the same work history competing
for the same opportunity (sometimes an absurd mental
laboratory is useful). The candidates happen to be identical
twins with essentially the same mannerisms, character,
initiative and so on, separated by only one distinction. One
twin has developed his descriptive writing skills to an art
form whereas his brother really considered writing a pain-
in-the-ass. Now the lobotomy test question…which bro
gets the interview after posting a cover letter and resume?

Even if you're slow you see where I am going. All things
being equal your ability to describe (and to a large extent,
embellish) your work history will place you in front.
Embellish, as I've used it, does not imply falsifying. No,
many people are so bland in describing what they've done.
As a reader, pulling the material benefit your employer has
derived from you is absent. In a perfunctory manner many
people limit resume entries to functional aspects of past
work without the "so-what?" They fail to tell the reader
how their employer benefited. It's o.k. to brag a little!
You need to! Don't go overboard, but there is some reason
your previous or current employer keeps you around.
Figure out what your impact was and talk about it.

The current rage (it's been the gold-standard for over a
decade) is to begin resume bullet statements with action
words such as "Managed" or "Negotiated". That approach
is o.k. but everyone uses it. If you want to introduce a
refreshing changeup talk about how your company profited
from having you around.

Your resume should include a pre-amble that is essentially a summary of accomplishments…it's usually entitled "professional summary". How you present yourself via appearance, spoken word, attitude, and finally in the written form paints a picture by which you will be judged worthy of additional pursuit.

7) Your age – I'm not supposed to talk about this am I? At the time of this writing I am forty-six. While not old yet I've been precocious and no longer am. I can write with a degree of authority on how perceptions are affected. H.R. responses really annoy me because there is truth on the one hand and then the pat reading of policy on the other. The former is veiled and the latter is posted. Think this one doesn't have influence? As the work-force ages you'd best learn how to play this. It can be an advantage or it can have a department trying to take you down.
In general I think the paranoia surrounding "getting old" is overstated.

The truly funny thing is that we hear often of the discrimination against older workers. I recall years ago having to overcome perceptions that I didn't know what the hell I was talking about given my youth. Now, there is assumed authority in much that I say given title, age, experience and so on.

When you hire a consultant you want to see gray hair. You want to know that you've got the best in the field. The assumption is that to gain the status "expert" you need to have done something long enough to really understand it as no one else does. This fact is quite the opposite of the perception that older workers are washed up. What's real?

Obviously nose hairs, ear hairs, a lack of it on the head, those things which belie one's age also detract from youthful beauty. Youthful beauty is wonderful! It should be celebrated! I love beer commercials! Always have.

Now, to the actual discrimination. If you are interviewing for a beer commercial I really don't want to see liver-spots and saggy…you-know-what. Taking the reality pill on things age-wise, there are places and times where discrimination is valid. Seventy year-old firemen, eighty year-old cocktail waitresses, are certainly the extreme examples. I will tell you though that by-and-large, where expertise is truly valued, age discrimination is harder to find than you might be led to believe. Some will crucify me for what I am saying. Simply put, if you carry yourself well, you have good energy, and you really do shine in a specific field people will respond well to you. The steel company I work for employs engineers who have both the money and the experience to hang it up. These are people we are honored to have around because simply put they don't need us! We use them to train younger engineers and condense their "learning curve" a bit. They have tremendous value that you can't learn overnight. Discrimination?

Yes, I get it, there are people who fall victim to the notion that only the young and energetic are worth the investment of time. Such a position is usually self-limiting. Back to my reference in the first paragraph. Yes, I concede there are fields where discrimination is borne out by statistics. Software development. How many of the "worker-bees" and management staff are over fifty? Unless you are an owner you may want to steer away from the whole I.T. thing. Bias in this realm is real. For other industries, however, this doesn't seem to be the case.

Granted, there may be professions where the path to proficiency is long and you might avoid investing tremendous time in training someone who is near retirement but I truly believe that common outcries of age discrimination "you can't get hired if you're over fifty!" are largely invalid. Now is the time I will get bombarded with hate mail.

Looking at the upcoming shortage of experience in the power industry, waste-treatment, heavy industrial fields, petroleum refining and exploration, and a host of light manufacturing fields, I struggle with any notion that you "can't" find work at a certain age given many companies are trying to figure out how to delay impending retirement of their older/experienced workforce.

People will judge you in a complete package including your age - your age is only one item that enters their perception. Whether it serves to your advantage or to eliminate consideration rests largely with how you present yourself. We are superficial as a species. You may be older but if you are also in shape, smile, show energy, truly bring subject matter expertise to bear, and you lead well, guess what? All that other crap? Gone! Now, if you are plugging for a lower-level staff position competing with others much younger and offering nothing more? See 'ya! Those are the cold and cruel facts. I'll say this, though. If you are older I would hope you have something to offer that either offsets or is enhanced by your age. And if you harbor resentment and bitterness that you are being overlooked while trying to compete head-to-head with the younger generation I can only help you by saying "drop it!" Find that area where you can offer more and pursue that! Being a grouch will only reinforce the stereotype.

Now that I have the AARP ready to hunt me down let me suggest they study the revised unemployment statistics. Ain't Grannie that's losing her job! The youth, or those most recently graduated are having one hell of a time finding work. Getting that foot in the door seems to be a huge problem. Especially when many younger folks are attending college without really drilling down on what will get them hired.

Age discrimination implies bypassing older workers. I can make a case that age discrimination is more likely dismissing recent graduates as inexperienced. The fact is, if you are a college student hoping to land a job after earning your degree, you might want to fight for any relevant internship you can find immediately! The current economy is hardly friendly to anyone requiring training. You will want to demonstrate as well as you are able that you can bring value to an organization from the start. Certainly you want to speak to your potential but you can learn things today that will help your case.

For younger workers the choice of study will have a huge bearing on your initial chances. As I've discussed before, certain technical fields will fair well. In general fine arts and journalism are a sucker's bet. I'll see you at Hallmark when I'm shopping for cards. Even a "business" undergraduate degree is arguably a waste of your time. The sciences, math, engineering, and nursing will give you something of value at the undergraduate level. As for graduate and professional school I would only encourage the overrated MBA as an adjunct to a career as opposed to a stand-alone. Medicine, specialized facets of law (patent law and environmental law are good), actuarial science (graduate math studies with an emphasis on statistics), advance engineering degrees, these will put beans on the table. Again, I'm not discounting the intrinsic merits of studying language, music, art, literature, history, etc. but this is a book about finding work. Another life's lesson. If you can pay your bills you actually can focus on areas of enjoyment in ways that you cannot when you are about to be evicted from your apartment. Fancy yourself a musician? My advice…work in a dissimilar lucrative field, buy yourself a sound studio, and spend time at home practicing away! Get an additional degree in music if you wish but for God's Sake, don't count on your whims to feed you. The pitfall of the young is to wax ideal and ignore fiscal matters. Get the money straight and the more rewarding pursuits will be yours to chase without distraction. Enough on age.

8) Projecting confidence – this seems to be the inherent trait of a lucky few but trust me when I tell you it can be learned. The lack of confidence projected by shifty looks at one's feet, hands in pockets, drooped shoulders, over-apologizing, too many qualifiers in your answers, lack of eye contact, stammering, etc. kills chances of consideration. It's a poison.

If you know that you have opportunity to improve on this let me help. Understanding and having rehearsed your message prior to interviewing will help more than any single "trick". A technique I used in my youth while I was somewhat intimidated by people in power – I tried answering concisely and holding eye contact after finishing my thought. I smiled and answered the question and no more. Get comfortable with the pause. The key is finish your thought! Nervous Nellies don't. They ramble. God help me they ramble. Now that I sit opposite the interviewee (sometimes in panel format, sometimes alone) I want to scream out to candidates "Don't talk past the sale!" For some reason when people are nervous or lack conviction they blow the deal by talking when they shouldn't. Learn to listen, collect your thoughts, and answer clearly and with economy of words. Better short and to-the-point than wandering.

Smile! Make eye contact. Ask questions of your own. Breathe! Sit upright. Butterflies and a touch of nerves are good. Run with it. But rehearse, prepare, study typical interview questions in the next chapter, practice aloud your answers, and you will help yourself.

This is a horribly brief rundown on presenting yourself. You know most of this. I will describe specifics regarding making contacts and interviewing in following chapters. Now I'd like to talk about the psychology of the process. Interviewing as it stands can be a very unnatural and weird process. Shopping for candidates is typically too brief a process for the interviewer, and awkward to intimidating for the interviewee. It's not something you generally look forward to. The tone of the proceedings varies tremendously whether you are responding to a posted job or if you created an opportunity/sold and idea to a company and now you're just cinching the deal. The latter is ideal whereas the former places you in the position of having to differentiate from the pack. I want to discuss the potential mood in a matrix of scenarios and how best to work through each. A quick notice on vernacular...I reference the role "Hiring Manager" often in this book. Simply put this is the person making the final hiring decision and would typically be your future boss.

Scenario A – Your interview followed from a posting – competing with the masses. In this case you have written a compelling cover letter, your background seems to fit as presented on your resume and your phone interview went well. A date is set for your first in-person interview. Two key potential formats here. The first is the best. You will be briefed by an H.R. representative and then meet with the hiring manager. The second sub-category is a panel interview. Potential boss/department peers/others will assess you in one or more rounds of group interviews. In this case it's easy to feel like you're subject to interrogation. The panel interview is the most awkward and stupid format but many human resource departments live by it.

In either case you are following a procedure somewhat laid out by a human resources department with input from the hiring manager. A need was assessed in the company, a requisition was approved, and now in a formal way they are out to find as close to what it is they are "looking for". In most cases each participant has a different view of what that is. Generally the hiring manager will fill out a form describing to the best of his/her ability just what the qualifications and functional needs are. Funny thing you need to be clear on - in many cases qualifications are highly negotiable if

you have similar experience and/or can describe how you will
address said qualifications. Do not shy away from pursuing a job
if everything doesn't match up perfectly. It never does. The
company will simply try, as closely as they are able, to get the best
amalgam of "as close to" qualifications as they can get along with
less tangible attributes (as they assess) such as drive, energy,
personality, etc. The latter are often more important in any
interview process.

Under this scenario you are responding to a need a company feels
they have. Duh! You are not necessarily matching the opening up
with any need you have other than to find work. Please, for your
sanity, evaluate whether or not the advertised position to which
you are responding tangibly meets or can be morphed to address
your career goals. It's gotta' work both ways. The probability of a
good marriage here is slim. Nonetheless, if it's early in your career
or you simply need to have a job related to your background that's
o.k. Every one of us will be in this situation at some point.

Now, even though there is a job description complete with posting,
you still need to work your due-diligence on what the company is
truly after. The phone interview coupled with some of your own
research should shed light on what the company wants. Is the
opening a result of expansion? Perhaps a new contract? What
about attrition or firing? Ultimately how does the advertised
position effect the company's profitability? Can you paint this
picture? At times the people interviewing are not prepared to
articulate the same – if you are able you will make one hell of a
good impression.

We'll assume an internal candidate is not in the picture and the
interview is sincere. Too often a posting along with limited
external interviews are carried out for compliance reasons – that's
a massive waste of everyone's time. If you are meeting one-on-
one with the hiring manager you will enter a forum where it is
easier to communicate who you are and craft the presentation you
would like. It's a classic "give-and-take" format. In this instance
you have a chance to sell yourself directly to the strongest voice in

the vote. The hiring manager is evaluating how you will interact with him/her and if it's a "thumbs-up", that will usually be communicated to others who may interview you separately later…try telling the boss he's full of crap! The others will typically agree.

If you will be interviewed in a panel format you will need to prepare carefully. Panel interviews often leave you feeling awkward and uncertain how you came across. Usually these will be carefully scripted with the interviewer having a list of questions of which each panel member must ask a few. In this forum getting nods from most or all will be tricky. You've got different personalities, roles, and perceptions. Number one - do not appear intimidated. Project friendliness and openness at all times. Whoever asks a question make certain that you answer by making eye contact with all. Rule number one for any interview - make damned sure you understand the question before trying to answer. If you need clarification, ask! In this situation there is the least allowance for straying from the question. Be concise but not truncated. Many of the canned questions will be annoying. Answer them politely and quickly. Allow them time to write their notes. Don't be put off by the silence. Smile. Amuse yourself with how stupid this process can be. Check every now and then by asking "does that answer your question?" or some variant thereof. After the barrage of them asking you countless tiring questions and writing there is always a slot of time for your questions. The conventional wisdom is that you had better have questions. Guess what? You'd better have questions. But this is your time to shine if you've prepped well. You will go into the interview with a story of what you understand the position to be and how you will improve upon it. You will begin by throwing out questions of what they perceive the position to entail. Do not ask what type of person they are looking for. Ask instead how they view the role. You will be surprised at the lack of continuity between respondents. If they are smart they will defer the question to the hiring manager.

Once the panel is silent on how they view the open role it's time to paint your picture of how you would take on the role. If you've prepared a story-line on how you would improve the company through the advertised job, this is where you tell it. Begin by recounting what the interviewers shared about the job and add your own view if not radically different. Talk about what can be improved and how you will work with others to make it happen. Not you alone, companies are very sensitive to "team". Describe the functional aspects that need to happen and how you, with others, will drive results. Mention specific improvements that you envision. Ask the panel members if they feel this would benefit the company. Even if your perceptions of the job are a little off from reality, it doesn't matter. You've made the effort to think through how you will enhance the position and benefit the company. Guess how few candidates do this? Even at a high level, very few. Frighteningly few. It's as if people have forgotten how to sell. Somewhere in the conversation you need to build the idea that you have vision and your vision will bring profit to someone. So what if your role is low-level engineering. Don't be afraid to impress someone. This is not the time for modesty. Au contraire – by explaining how your results will improve the business you are showing more business acumen than the "position" would call for and to some extent you may be interviewing for a future promotion.

The close. It ain't carried out in the conference room. To cover the elementary aspects… DO NOT ASK ABOUT SALARY DURING THE FIRST FACE-TO-FACE! Ever! If the hiring manager asks you over the phone or one-on-one for screening purposes they will usually ask "What are you making now?". Though they can find out on your W-2 from prior year you must not simply blurt out how much. You can deftly float a number or a range that you are looking for and remind him/her that if that's close then salary can be worked out once a fit is determined. The "ought-to" at the close of the interview is to ask about the next step. This might be dodged but it shows your engagement. Closing the deal is the follow-up. Assuming you want to go further make sure that you've gotten everyone's name, email, mail address, etc. You will draft hardcopy letters to each thanking them for the interview and telling them how much you look forward to a next discussion opportunity. Again, you'd be surprised how few candidates follow-up.

I don't offer much advice on subsequent phases. This will likely narrow in on a final discussion or two between you and a future boss. Discussions will move to the specific. Salary negotiations are carried out from this time forward. Notice I said negotiations. If they insist on asking how much you make, that's fine, tell them. Remind them, though that you are looking for improved opportunity. If you're not working then you have no leverage. Don't engage in truly tough negotiations if you can't afford to walk.

There is your superficial how-to for answering a posting. Remember, this is not the ideal method of finding a career. Explanation to follow how you can create the ideal opportunity…one you identify and sell to a company. Imagine interviewing for a position you helped create.

<u>Scenario B</u> – A headhunter catches you at the right moment…advice on the process to follow.

O.k. so this should be closer to a hand-and-glove fit than Scenario A, right? Clearly you're developed professionally and people know who you are. A headhunter would not waste your time if she didn't think you were a match…of course not!

Even though headhunters are hired by their client, the hiring company, if they can get you past ninety days on the job, they collect a fee equivalent to one third the value of your first year's salary. Not bad for a short-term incentive. The concern for a perfect fit is less than you think.

The odds may be slightly improved in your favor toward something you might actually enjoy and advance your career but they are still dim. If indeed you are exploring the idea of leaving your current job and you have no clear direction I advise you at least see if you can get an interview. Learning about the opportunity is harmless. Practice interviewing is never a loss. You might lose one day of vacation but you'll learn something at the least. Just enter with an open mind and don't expect too much.

The dynamics in this circumstance are more favorable than answering an ad. A company is putting up sincere money to get the right candidate. They will be choosy but the field will be small and the need is real. As much scrutiny as you may seem subject to, remember, you were the one contacted. You need them less than they need you. Cliché? Perhaps but that's reality. They are investing money and have given more than casual thought to who they are looking for. The company is serious.

Here is how the scenario will play out. You get the call from the headhunter. After some probing questions you're asked to send in your resume. At this point cursory questions only have been asked about your background but there seems to be enough of a fit to pursue. Most often you will receive calls to fill a role in precisely the same industry doing the same thing. If that's all there is to it than skip it. Your interest lies in bettering your circumstance. Do not violate cardinal rule #1 – never make a move that does not materially benefit your income by at least 20% and/or lead to increased responsibility. If the headhunter is trying to fill a role that might be a stretch for you then stretch! She may be less-than-enthusiastic but you must try. Those deemed precocious versus those who never seem to move ahead are often separated only by the fact that they tried. Calculated aggressiveness is rewarded. We are taught to be humble at home and there is a time for it but assertiveness rules in the workplace. It's seldom punished.

Obviously the headhunter is the gatekeeper. In some cases you meet, in others it's simply a phone process before you are given the name and number of the hiring manager – in this instance it's almost a shoe-in that you will be speaking to a perspective boss. If the hiring manager is still interested after reading your resume you can view the a phone interview as yours to louse up. You've cleared the highest hurdle. Assuming you're compliant with the self-help tips mentioned at the beginning of this chapter and your mannerism on the phone is good, contain your nerves at all costs and begin selling yourself...tactically.

Before the phone interview, do as I will repeat exhaustively throughout this writing – prepare! Mechanically obvious is to scour the company website. Don't stop there, research the markets the company is in. Products, services, research competitors! Google the CEO. Find out from any angle you can every scrap of information you can about the company. This exercise will either support your interest or cause you to pursue something else. Remember, we're talking about your career here. Now, here comes the effort. After gathering everything you can, figure out how the role the company is looking to fill might impact profitability. Articulate it to yourself. Say it. Get used to saying it. Clarify in your mind how the company might improve their status in their target markets. Focus on the job's impact to company growth and/or profitability. "Well Mr. Author, what if I'm trying to become an H.R. Supervisor? How the hell does that tie to profitability?" Figure it out! Using this example, it's easy. An H.R. Supervisor plays a role in the hiring practices. Getting shitty people means shitty results. Focus on the flip-side. If you're going to work as an actuary for an insurance company, the accuracy of your modeling will influence profitability directly. If premiums don't match risk you're screwed! Salespeople don't need help with this discussion – you'd better know. Regulatory folks may find this exercise more difficult but there is still a story to tell. Negotiating most favorable permitting or helping to guide the company's best choice weighing product market potential versus laboratory testing costs can be part of your story. Figure it out and get prepared to tell it.

Here's where the psychology must be played well. Understand that you are now at a point where the hiring manager is intrigued. Unless you entirely fuck-up the call he is in a buying mood even if he presents a you're-lucky-to-be-talking-to-me face. That's most often the case. Let the dance begin but if you are this far along, remember, for whatever reason, he has bought into the notion that there are only a very select few who stand a chance of succeeding in the open position. Vascular surgery and propulsion nozzle design aside, it's likely the field of potential candidates is broader than he imagines. Don't ruin the moment. Feed the illusion. Where you don't offer precise experience defer to similar accomplishments. Emphasize your aptitude – your ability to learn. Most importantly, at the appropriate time, share the exercise I pushed in the preceding paragraph. Preface with a scenario about how you view the company's profit and/or growth goals, confirm, and then share your vision on what you would do to help the larger goal…not simply fulfilling the stated position objectives. Tie in for the hiring manager how you would use your skills and talents to bolster the company objectives through the open position. Remember when I said to "confirm"? What if your scenario is wrong? Oh my God! Mission aborted, right? Nope. By asking if your understanding of the company goals are close or half-baked you will already have demonstrated an uncommon interest and opened the door to be told what those objectives are. Either you're close and your prepared story works or you're off, to be corrected, and you can still paint a picture of how you will support the goals.

This approach detracts from the time-honored and nauseating practice of allowing the hiring manager to pick apart your history and explain to you why you haven't done the kinds of things this position will demand. That is so much bullshit and the exercise can be stopped by you! You can guide the conversation once he allows you to speak. Aside from professional licensure requirements, very seldom does anyone's specific background most qualify them to succeed. Perhaps it means they have an easier ramp-up period to perform the minimal expectations but by waging the argument described above you've completely trashed the traditional rationale. You've now painted a picture in his mind that he might not have considered. He's shifted from trying to play matchmaker to seeing potential he didn't consider. Wow! You're good! This works! Remember when I said I've nearly always been hired?

You're not finished. You've done more than merely pique his interest. You've told a compelling story. If done well you've somewhat redrafted the job description to better fit you. Now it's time to meet in person. You still might see variations of how the in-person interview is conducted as discussed under Scenario A, yet the mood will be far different. Whether you are just meeting with a future potential boss alone or with others the setup is in your favor. There is still a deal to be closed so let's get to that.

Before the first face-to-face continue to study the company and learn about the things you don't know. Related processes, customers, competitors, markets, products, services, and they way they sell to their customer base. Continue to think about how you will help the company succeed in light of what they do and where they are headed. This is a legitimate approach. What if you get the job? Your path will be far clearer. Imagine how impressed those involved in the interview will be if you walk in with a plan. This plan should speak to how you will carry out the job in the first ninety days, the first six months, and in the long-term. Stunning approach, huh? You might think this approach is presumptuous. You risk more by not having a plan than communicating a plan that the interviewers don't deem the perfect plan. You can manage the potential to appear presumptuous by stopping periodically and asking what is important to the company and incorporating that in your approach. The most frequent failure is someone arriving at an interview presenting their background, and allowing the interviewers to connect the dots. Even professional sales people, folks who live daily by painting a story, selling benefits, and explaining to customers how their approach will boost the customer's profit or savings, seem to derail when it comes to selling their own story.

A note of etiquette in selling your story – clearly you want to communicate that you have a plan and talk about what you think your approach will offer the company at a higher level. What I mean by a "higher level" is simply how a company/ division/ department will see improved financials from your effort. This does several things: 1) You are now viewed as a strategic thinker.

2) You've communicated to management you understand what's important to the company. 3) You have connected the dots for your listeners so they won't be left to the task – avoiding a dangerous proposition. Again, you will want to confirm your vision and ask along the way what is important to them. In this way you will offer a more compelling view of how you will help.

Wrap-up time – as you conclude your in-person interview you will always want to confirm both your interest and it's o.k. to ask how your plan gels with their needs. Always ask about the vaunted "next step" even though they'll likely dodge with a "we'll get back with you". You still need to ask.

As with every in-person interview follow-up is a must. My preference is that you send each a polite email and hardcopy. A short note that thanks them and reminds them of what you would like to bring to the position.

Generally at this point you will be able to read whether there is a strong interest or not. If you are called back it is usually a formality.

<u>Scenario C</u> – You read an internal posting = advancement opportunity and you want to move up in the organization you work for. This seems like a great fit!

It's nice that you get to see internal postings before they are available to the Public – right? Careful on this one – many people work for large organizations that cover multiple product and service disciplines and geographies. It's tempting to regard yourself as somehow advantaged.

If you're lucky the Hiring Manager in this case knows you and thinks well of you. It's more likely these days that you are anonymous. Finding an internal someone of mutual acquaintance who is willing to plug for you and whose opinion will be regarded highly is critical. If you cannot arrange this than you may as well skip the effort because I can nearly guarantee that someone in the company has this advantage. You need it.

The second and more important point that you will have to navigate is often unanticipated. If this opportunity is important to you and there is time between right now and when you will begin the interviewing process there is a matter of initiative you must demonstrate – this is absolutely critical. You must contact those in the department you would like to work for and see if you can arrange time to sit with potential co-workers to learn as much as you can. If you cannot be physically there then try calling people in key roles and interviewing them! Ask them to describe as well as they can what would be involved, they type of person they would like to see get the job, and ask what is most important to them. The best scenario would be if the opportunity is local and you can ask permission to spend time with the people and learning something of the process prior to interview time.

If I seem adamant on the prior point allow me to explain. Having participated as an interviewer for many internal candidates here are some observations:

1) Many internal candidates wrongly assume they've got the edge because they "know people". They skip the formal explanation of how they would benefit the position and almost to a point of being rude they don't know much about the department to which they've applied.
2) A common set of questions for an internal candidate goes something like this.
Q1 – "So, this opportunity is very important to you, right?"
Q2 – "Tell me, if this is so important, what have you done to demonstrate your interest level or learn about the job?

Q3 – "Can you give us an example of how you took
time from your schedule to learn about the department
or spend time with the people you might want to work
with?

Only twice in over thirty interviews have I been impressed with
someone who did in fact endeavor to learn about the people, the
department, and the position. This apparently elementary point is
most often missed. Act like you are a hungry external candidate
with the advantage of access to details and external candidate does
not have. If you cannot make the effort to learn everything you
can then sitting for an interview comes off as almost arrogant. The
expectation that you are "in the good" because the same logo
appears on your paycheck is flawed. Show double the initiative!

Have I mentioned networking? Oh yeah! Internally? But why?
Works here too! Don't forget it. Call it politics, call it whatever
you wish but you need to have good "influencers". Being known
for the right reasons will help you with internal postings,
advancement, and created opportunity. Blatantly obvious but don't
forget or take this one for granted.

Consistent with every scenario I present you must research what is
most valuable to the hiring manager, make sure it clicks with your
skills and interests, and then paint the picture very clearly to those
in the position to hire why they need you! You will develop a plan
and then explain it. The fact you are an internal candidate can
either sabotage you (lull you into inaction and gross assumptions)
or you can seize information and access advantage outsiders do not
have to get information and paint your picture. The last obvious
item was mentioned before…find someone of mutual acquaintance
who will vouch for you if you are largely unknown to the people
you will talk with.

Scenario D – **You decide what you want to do and who you
want to work for. You create a position.**

Are you kidding me? This steps outside traditional bounds yet it is the most effective in terms of career satisfaction and getting you hired. It also takes the most up-front work, time, research, networking, and introspection. Lastly, you must sell yourself to someone who does not realize how they might profit from what you can do for them. It takes vision, spine, lots of work, salesmanship, and tenacity. This is why it's seldom done. You can already tell I am going to highly recommend this for you. If you succeed in this approach your career trajectory will be defined by you. It is worth every fraction of sweat, nerves, and time that you will invest.

A few questions for you... What is the likelihood that someone else's immediate need represents a great fit for you? How often do over-defined staff positions offer the career potential that you are looking for? How much competition do you think you will have for a posted position? How much competition do you think you will have for a position where you get to write the job specifications? Mull this over. This is a huge departure from the want-ads, headhunters, and traditional means of searching.

I used the word "introspection". This is where you need to be very clear. It shouldn't take the most time but don't fuel this effort without being clear on what you want to do. A qualifying remark or two. Obviously many companies predefine positions. They have only specific functions listed in engineering, procurement, human resources, product development, sales, information-technologies, and so on. Many companies essentially have an org-chart and little latitude to "invent a position" so to speak. Even in these cases, if you contact the right person (CEO, Department Manager, Plant Manager, etc) and sell your story well, you may end up with a predefined title, but you will have created an opportunity. Generally the larger the company, the less latitude you will find in title. Don't omit them simply because of a rigid HR structure. Smaller companies tend to have more latitude in title and creating a position once sold. In either case you are presenting yourself to a person. Sell your idea well and an opportunity will be created for you. In some cases it takes more bureaucratic wrangling than in others but once the right person wants you aboard it doesn't matter.

Back to you. You are an amalgam of experience, ability, and initiative. The latter two are generally far more important than the first. H.R. departments focus on the first. Your job is to sell the latter two to the right person. But first, you must make an honest assessment of what you'd like your career to look like before you go any further. This is not simple. For example, does your education tend to "pigeon-hole" you? You are bright enough to figure out if there are any defacto exclusions between your desired career and your background. Assuming you will chase those opportunities where this is not an issue you can create an opportunity for yourself far better than an anonymous job opening. The most important part of this exercise is to decide what you'd like to do and how far you wish to take it. This endeavor assumes you have reached a maturity level where you understand basic profitability drivers for a company and how your chosen career will deliver benefit. To an extent this is rehash advice from foregoing sections with one twist. In this scenario you will have to understand your direction more clearly and your impact to a company in more detail than previously. Also, your "sales strategy" is different and I will carefully lay it out for you. You will choose the company, the job, the job description, who you will report to, and how your career will grow in subsequent years.

It's best if I give you a concrete example using specific narrative. The career-path is not as important as the approach. It may be applied whether you are pursuing journalism or supply-chain-logistics.

I'll use one of my own examples as a first case. I was working as a corporate account manager for 3M. Great career and solid compensation. I had accumulated decent vacation and benefits. Why in the hell would I ever consider leaving? Only for something that more directly suited my career objectives. My position at 3M was really a carryover from two acquisitions. I had started working as a National Account Manager for a small filtration company. I loved the job! Mostly I loved the culture! We were a small $35MM company growing quickly. Any "job" you had was truly fluid. Nothing was clearly defined. It was an "all-hands-on-deck" mentality and a nice blend of talent that allowed us to meet customer requirements quickly, take market share, and develop new products more quickly than in highly structured environments. The mood was intoxicating. The company was in fact publicly owned and had reached the point where the Management Team wished to sell. They did. At first to a mid-sized publicly owned company and then a year later that company was acquired by 3M. The atmosphere changed. It wasn't bad per se, but the focus shifted to product line profitability within the context of greater 3M versus meeting customer requirements and taking market-share. New customer opportunities were harder to sell internally than the external sell. Many hours were spent evaluating legal exposure and regulatory risk. I understood a risk-managed approach but it seemed there were three people paid to tell me why we could not pursue opportunity for every person seeking it. Enthusiasm quickly gave way to frustration.

During this time I knew of a large steel company called Nucor. The name was not new to me or how they conducted business. They were large, approaching $15B in sales in 2005, but somehow they managed keep that "entrepreneurial fire". Their compensation structure was unique. If the company did well, the "Team Members" did well. If the company faired poorly, so did everyone. Risky, yet connected. In this way those who worked for Nucor were not a managed expense.

I had a lengthy education as a mechanical engineer working with water systems. In fact, to keep my skills sharp, I moonlighted occasionally. I wanted to keep my engineering license and my skills current. Now and then I would accept a moonlighting project related to water systems design. None of this applied to my work with 3M so there was no conflict of interest. Nucor generally promoted from within. I wanted to join Nucor but did not want to start at ground level. Competition to get in to Nucor was extreme

and I really did not know anyone "high up". Here is what I
decided to do. I knew people who contracted with Nucor and an
engineer working directly for the company. I presented them with
information specific to my moonlighting efforts and asked if they
would name drop at the appropriate time. They did. After about
six months I was given the opportunity to do a small project for
them. This started a relationship with the company that grew. I
ended up working projects for a total of four of their facilities.
Now I was connected with people at four facility locations and a
General Manager at their corporate location. All while continuing
to work successfully at 3M.

My Nucor corporate contact had actually opened the door for me
relative to working directly for the company instead of consulting.
Nothing was directly offered but it was mentioned. That was all I
needed. The time came when I was really unhappy with my
situation at 3M and I called him. He could not hire me directly but
knew what I could do for the company and put me in touch with
the General Manager of a steel mill. They had an opening for a
Department Manager - a position that had been vacant for a year.
My background on paper did not appear to prepare me for this
position. It showed a solid technical background, good
management attributes, but no recent department management nor
development of employees. Though I had never run a department
and my current position had no direct reports, I had help from
inside. Strong allies within the company, people who could vouch
for my technical acumen and people skills, vouched for me. I
understood what was required for this position as I had been doing
project work directly for four such individuals with Nucor (all
recommending me for this job).

Later I found out that Nucor had already started trying to fill the
position through their network of headhunters. They were not
meeting with success. The requirements of this position,
Environmental Manager, were superficially light years away from
what I was involved with at 3M. Yet I knew I could excel in the
position. Try explaining that to a headhunter making their living
trying to find a round peg for a round hole. My resume did not

read very closely to the position. I would never have been glanced at taking a traditional approach. As it turned out I had every advantage over an external candidate with all of the "right" qualifications. My internal recommendations coupled with the fact that I could articulate the requirements of the position and how I might improve upon it. No genius at work here. I simply took on minor project work for the company, got to understand the business and more importantly gained the trust of people who worked there. Done. Granted, personnel at this particular steel mill did not know me but the support of Team Members from sister divisions gave me quite the credibility lift that got me to the interview.

Skipping the interim details, I was hired. Case closed. I am not suggesting that you moonlight as a means of gaining employment with a target company but my experience shows you one non-traditional means of getting in the door. In so doing I had every bit as much credibility as a true internal candidate. Nucor looked at me quite differently than a headhunter referral (not to mention they avoided the headhunter fee).

Key things to learn: a) Prior experience does not lock you in to a specific career-path. b) You must identify a target career and how you will fit. c) Crystallize in your mind how you will make a company more profitable. d) Identify who or what type of person within the organization you need to sell your story to. e) Infiltrating a target organization is not easy. Obviously you can "cold-call". I don't recommend this. You are seldom removed by more than three people from a contact in a company you wish to work for. You "know people who know people". Ask around. You will find someone in the company. See if you know anyone who provides services to the target company.

Chapter Five – Interviewing Basics

Now that you are familiar with a few interviewing formats/scenarios it's time to dig into the "how". Preparation for typical lines of questioning is often glossed over by candidates. You will prepare! Study carefully upcoming typical interview questions and suggested answer patterns. This will serve you well. First, though, you will find a few words on interview etiquette.

The initial phone interview

I'll start with the phone screen. For this discussion let's skip the headhunter screen and hit the actual phone interview with a prospective employer. Again, how you got to this point varies but there will be similar goals for the hiring company. The key goal of the phone interview is to start getting a sense of who you are but more importantly to weed you out based on crude criteria. This will not be the "deep probe". Instead, it's typical to confirm if you are willing to relocate, discuss your background a bit more in depth, make sure there is nothing fatal in your history that would exclude you from consideration, and see how you conduct yourself. This is not an appropriate time for the hard sell. However, there are leading remarks you can make and questions you can ask them that will fester and grow to the point you'll likely get to the next step.

My "Golden-Rule" again – you must know who the company is, what they do, the markets they serve, how the open position will impact the company's profitability, who the competitors are, and get a sense of who they might be looking for and the concerns they may have. All of this in advance! Not easy, I know, but the web is a good start, as are people you know who may know someone in the company. If it's a public firm there is so much you can review online. Private may be a bit harder but you can study what they do and likely they will be competing against a public firm. I'll offer more on researching a company later but for now let's assume you've done your homework prior to the call.

What you will do is allow the interviewer to structure the interview. Do not get stupidly eager and cut the person off or prevent her from finishing sentences. You must be smooth. Contain your enthusiasm. The beginning of the call is usually fairly scripted. Answer each question concisely. It's critically important that you do not ramble on the phone. It's effective to ask if you've answered her question but end your thought! Midway through the call things tend to loosen up a bit. Now is when you can subtly roll out those little punch lines. Here's what I mean. Let's say the job is in the deep-south and you are located in Chicago. An anticipated concern is that you are not going to be happy. They won't ask directly about your living preferences but as the conversation allows you to ask questions why not ask something like…"do they have good bass fishing nearby?" Assuming of course you've learned the location and you know it to be so. Fire a leading question that reveals a hobby or a want of yours that can be addressed by the area. Maybe there is a concern relative to your education level. Again, a question about local educational opportunities may table the idea that you intend to go further. This sounds a little deceptive but if you are honest and you can identify something about the job or the location that you might enjoy and you are able to reveal this in an off-hand way it can be very effective.

You must also have questions. Again, this is a two-way street. This is a screening call for you too. I'll tell you repeatedly that you do not want to negotiate terms and salary early in the game but you will want to make sure neither of you are wasting time. Explain to them in all candor you just want to make sure that you are not out of line and mention rough target compensation. If prefaced honestly then no harm. You will want to ask directly what kind of person they are looking for and why the position is available. Eventually you will want to offer something about your background that is clearly enticing to them and ask if that attribute would be helpful? You don't want oversell here. Once the "sniffing out" is accomplished and no one is hanging up the phone, ask if you can have the in-person interview if you've not already been asked.

A phone screen should last no more than thirty minutes. You want to reveal only enough to pique interest once you've cleared preliminary hurdles. Weave in little surprises about your understanding of the business, maybe people of mutual acquaintance, how the geographic area might suit you, basically you will throw seeds that should germinate if chosen well.

The initial "Face-to-Face"...traditionally the highest hurdle

As I preach in each chapter - research, research, research. Go back to the "Golden-Rule". In this meeting alone it is an imperative that you leave this interview having sold to your audience how you will deliver benefit to the position and in turn the company. This most obvious mission is ignored to the point of mystery even when interviewing for mid/upper management posts. I don't care if you are interviewing for grocery bagger. Set yourself apart. I guarantee someone with a close-to-perfect background who does not sell the message will lose by a wide margin to someone having an imperfect background who makes the sell. First-hand I've watched likeable candidates with plenty to offer leave it to me and/or the rest of the interview panel to pull facts and assimilate how the candidate might fit the job. You see there is this hidden assumption that the interviewer should take control from start to finish as they understand the needs of the position and you the interviewee are there to provide information as needed. Oooops!

Facts...a requisition was created but I would guarantee you not a single person interviewing will be able to articulate in crystal clear fashion the ideal candidate. They might try but I will submit there are many unconsidered approaches to doing the job very well. Further, when you add complexity of numbers on the interview panel you get discord. Ask the group who the ideal candidate might be and the wheels come of that train. Should you aim that question at the group, almost to a point of hilarity there will be sideways glances, and fumbling. Typically attempt one will be deferred to the hiring manager but there will be more clouds than clarity as each member weighs in. Even if it's a panel of one you will see hesitation.

So contrary to assumed convention the opportunity is wide open for you to share your view on how the position might develop and offer your approach and even risk sounding presumptuous as you talk about how the company will benefit from your approach. But do this having done your homework! As you discuss your vision check with your interviewer(s) to see if your assumptions are close – if you've researched well they will be. This requires discipline and planning. This is why so few do it. Most of us are along for the ride hoping we are special and the interview will flesh out the obvious. There are a number of reasons my own interviews have met with success. I've coached others and watched them nail the next opportunity. I'm nothing special – I simply plant in the listener's mind that I must be the right person for the job since I obviously have initiative, planning, and most often paint a thorough picture so they can see in advance how the plan brings value to the position. Almost as importantly, since they didn't truly have a clear picture on what the most successful approach might be, they accepted what was presented.

The temporal structure of an interview implies looking back on your experience. The fact is you need to bring your audience forward and explain what you will do. If you methodically approach opportunity this way and with integrity then you stand a better chance of finding a job you will like also. Think about it. If you're experiencing nausea in piecing together your story of how you will help, then likely you don't want to pursue.
The flip side – if you are becoming energized by putting your plan together you might just enjoy the job.

Now we move on to the interview. I've been discussing roughly how you will tell your story. Clearly you won't get to do this at the front of the interview. The historical probe of what you've done must come first. Cede control of the interview to the interviewer(s) when the process starts. Be mindful of the dos and don'ts that I discuss toward the end of this chapter. You will greet each interviewer and look them directly in the eye. You will be on time, you won't be flustered, you will be smooth, calm, pleasant, and damn it…smile! After introductions covering where to pee, checking to see if you want coffee, and all the formalities, I'd suggest you allow a bottle of water. Cotton-mouth never improved an interview.

As the interview reaches the right moment where you are invited to ask questions you may shift control and hit it out of the park. First, you must be prepared to wade through a barrage of questions. Tactics will vary but there are some conventional lines of questioning you will likely have to navigate. I detail them below and how you might respond.

Common generic questions and how best to answer:

Q1 – "Where do you see yourself in five years?"

In twenty years of being on one side of the interview desk or the other I cannot fathom what anyone can expect to gain in having a candidate work this one. Here is my best advice - simply answer that you see yourself as being successful in the role for which you are interviewing. Include the idea that at that point you hope to have developed viable replacements for your position in the event you are ready to move on. Do not follow the crappy advice some give that you see yourself in your future boss's role. There once was a time when stupid presumption and overaggressive behavior were thought to be desirable behavior traits. Don't. Stick to the script given.

Q2 – "What are your salary requirements?"

There are only two appropriate times to have this discussion. The first is a general inquiry in the first feel-out session to get an idea if the interview process is worth pursuing. The second is when you are the leading finalist and you are negotiating salary. If an interviewer is actually stupid enough to ask this in an initial face-to-face you need to simply state that you'd like to wait to see if there is a fit first and then negotiate if warranted. If they persist deflect again by mentioning that you are not clear yet if this is an opportunity of mutual interest. Once determined you will be in a better position to assess what a fitting salary ought to be.

Q3 – "Have you ever fired anyone?"

If so, discuss by covering only the relevant facts. Avoid any judgmental remarks. State clearly that you counseled the person, gave them every opportunity, and the individual essentially eliminated themselves. If it was a single event HR violation, so state, but again, the mood should be that the outcome was a last resort and unfortunate.

There are two hidden agendas here. The interviewer(s) are looking to see if you are rash or let emotion rule the moment. If a candidate seems gratified or happy that revenge was taken then game over. The second item that they might be looking for is to see what you learned. This might be revealed in your answer. If you were faced with someone who was poison to a department perhaps you learned that attitudes need to be addressed head-on. Perhaps you learned how to work the process so that the fired individual was not at all surprised when he was let go.

Q4 – "How would you gauge whether or not you were successful in this job?"

Because you have planned carefully how you will communicate benefit to this position and the unique plan you will present later in the interview, this one is simply handled by your discussing the benefit points you have prepared and using those as metrics. You will want to state those points and if you have achieved them you will be successful.

Q5 – "What qualities would the ideal candidate for this job possess?"

A variant of the above but with a twist. Here you will want to discuss character attributes that will allow the candidate to reach the objectives you came prepared to talk about. Formulate your answer by mentioning what a successful candidate would accomplish and then talk briefly about attributes that would help the person achieve those goals.

Q6 – "Describe the ideal boss."

I hear this one more often lately. It falls on my "Bull-Shit List" but be prepared nonetheless. First and foremost do not talk about character attributes on this one. You need to focus you answer on action bullets. Several are of key importance. You will want to state that the ideal boss would present clear expectations. You may want to mention that the expectations might be a result of agreed-upon goals the two of you (or the whole team) derived. Further, you will want to tell your audience that a great leader presents clear objectives for her department. She has expectations of you but also vision for where the department is going. A great boss will also give you the support needed to attain the expectations she has of you. She will also be a resource to help you develop as an employee. Lastly, she will hold those on her team accountable for meeting her expectations.

In so describing you've covered the generic highlights of a good leader. No need to go any further here.

Q7 – "If I were to call your boss and ask him to describe your weaknesses, what do you think he would say?"

This is annoying as hell yet you need to be prepared. There are several mutations of this question but somewhere in the process you're likely to get hit with this one. The transparent and most often used approach is to choose some attribute of you that might also be considered a strength. "He'll say I work too hard..." Oh, please! Shut up! Responses in that tone are so trite I advise instead that you honestly choose something not too damning but add to your answer what you are doing to improve this feature. The right type of honesty will win points. You don't want to reveal your alcoholism or your predisposition to yell at subordinates. Again, there is some relatively minor thing that you could improve upon. You will want to act like you're pondering the question but then go ahead and reveal this minor thing and then acknowledge the sin and talk a little about what you could do to improve upon it.

Q8 – "We all make mistakes. Tell me about a mistake you made in your career and what you learned."

Pretty self-explanatory – certainly have a scenario in mind prior to the interview and along with it, what you learned. If you feel you've had a spotless career, think again. Come up with something. The key that the interviewer will be zeroing in on is how you handled the mistake. What did you learn and how will you prevent it. A little humility on this one will win points. This can be a revealing exchange for anyone harboring ego issues. Own up and talk about what you took away and how it's made you better in your job/dealing with people. I've got to inject…don't use an example that will raise eyebrows. Do I need to add this? I guess I do! I've witnessed answers ranging from sexual impropriety ("it was really just a misunderstanding") to anger issues. Please keep this one vanilla.

Q9 – "In handling conflict with your supervisor, when do you feel it's appropriate to go to the next level in resolving it?"

Oh yes! Let's see if you'll throw your boss under the train! Please! I've never heard anyone get blatantly stupid with this. Yet…there are times people elaborate too much. Keep this one short and simple. It needs to be answered in this way,

"If we are at an impasse and she and I agree we cannot resolve the issue without her boss' help, then I would go with her approval. The only exception might be is if she's done something unethical."

The litmus test here is to ensure they are not about to hire anyone who freely circumvents the chain-of-command.

Q10 – "Why are you the right person for this job?"

So, why are you? You'd better articulate this to yourself before walking in. If you've worked your due-diligence and you know how you will benefit this company, explain it. Concise phrases and compact/powerful messages will earn you points. Your message needs to distill to something tangible. Quite simply you will bring a sales department more profit, you will engineer better profits allowing the company broader markets, you will slash costs and improve quality by running a better procurement department, your actuarial skills are so above-board you will prevent your employer from improperly allocating risk and losing money. Deliver the benefit and a very brief synopsis of how you will do this. Stay away from vague character attributes – no one gives a shit! Do not fumble in your answer! Know it, rehearse it, and believe it! If the question is never overtly asked provide the answer in some way. This is why you are here!

Q11 – "What brings you here today?"

In other words why are you interested in this position? I've provided likely variants of this question or closely related questions in Q10, Q12, and Q18. This opens the door to talk about why you are interested. All eyes will be on you. Appearing to contemplate this for the first time would be fatal. In fact you need to have given this enough thought that you can articulate clearly…without missing a beat.

Please for the love of God do not talk about "I really think it would be a great challenge". This cliché should cause immediate nausea among the interviewers.

Back to my advice on preparation – talk specifically about the needs of the job as you see them, your ability to provide those needs, and for personal motive discuss your desire to bring measurable improvement to a position. Think about how effective the response would be from the interviewer's perspective if you talk about wanting the job because you believe you can further the interests of the position hence the company! So elementary and so seldom thought of.

By the way...no one really cares about your wanting the position because of what it will do to round out your resume or because you feel you are ready to advance. Any self-assessment of grandeur is a put-off. The exception to talking about what it might do for you comes after you discuss how you intend to improve the position – then you can throw in the potential benefit to your career.

Q12 – "What can you do for us?"

I give you so many related examples because this is the crux of the interview. You'd better truly have this one down and memorized. More often than not, even in higher level management interviews, I've watched good candidates go up in smoke since they thought their experience spoke for itself. They failed to prepare a concise message of how they would meet the needs of the position. When the question came they fumbled the ball.

My same message again...this is your key opportunity question. Hit it over the fence. It's easy! I repeat – talk about how you see the needs of the position, discuss what your approach will be to bring improvement to the position, and perhaps provide examples of how you've done something similar. Practice (verbally) your message until you can preach it.

Q13 – "What makes you uniquely qualified for this position?"

In truth, nothing – statistically speaking you're no different than anyone else. Most candidates will talk about some aspect of their experience. I will tell you again, what you've done might be the deciding factor in brain surgery or programming but not in most pursuits. The "between the lines" question is really how dedicated will you be toward your role.

My advice goes something like this. Talk about the level of dedication you will bring to the position. Without comparing yourself to anyone, discuss your approach to business as treating other department members as customers. Talk about how hard you work in your current role to push toward department goals. You might even mention the hours you put in and that you never consider your career just a job.

Most interviewers will simply listen. Without overtly claiming to be superior you've cleared the hurdle simply by talking about character pluses you will bring to the position. Skip the specific experience – for the most part it doesn't matter much anyway other than to cover past wins to support your point.

Q14 – "Tell me about a weakness you have."

What the fuck? A repeat of Q7, right? Sort of. "O.k. Mr. Interviewer I publicly masturbate and exhibit Tourette Syndrome during customer meetings!" What do people hope to get from this moronic question? I hate this…yet it's often asked. Similar to the first two questions this is supposed to evoke exploration. Believe me the listener will be analyzing every word intently. This is a slight variant to Q7 – you can follow the advice there or go ahead with a non-cliché yet canned answer. Not too canned just your garden-variety revealing a harmless weakness or one that can spin into a strength. Careful not to sound too rehearsed. Be brief. Rehearse! Here's an example. "Well,…,I think maybe I can do a better job of delegating. I tend to involve myself at least a little in as many project details as I can. Ownership is great but I've got let go a little bit." This is not too obviously deflective. If they ask you about anything else then pause, pretend to ponder, and with a smile assure them nothing else comes to mind at the moment. Narcolepsy, anger issues, kleptomania, porn addictions, and the like are best omitted. Again, I'm assuming you, the reader, are bright.

Q15 – "What do you like to do in your free-time?"

The interviewer might honestly have a personal interest in you the candidate. They might also want to assess if you are boring or strange. Generally speaking this is a filler question with little consequence noted in the answer. Go ahead and share a not-so-weird hobby or two. Keep it vanilla and pleasant. Don't go wild with your war re-enacting or foam at the mouth in describing your confrontations at City Hall. Interviews have been killed here. Remember, pleasant and positive.

Q16 – "So, tell me about yourself."

This question or any wide open similar questions you need to turn it around on the interviewer before attempting to answer. Do not run with this one at face value. Respond with some variant of the following "What would you like to know about?" Open-ended questions are fine but good grief! How many thousand-page volumes do you think you would have to write to document everything that is you. The question is somewhat absurd as a stand alone. An intelligent response is to ask the interviewer to distill the question to help you answer it. Generally the interviewer has no other goal than to see where you will run with this. Confirm what topic to cover and then concisely cover it. If the interviewer leaves the topic to you then choose a business-related topic and make the narrative short. A good close would be, "is there anything else you wish to cover?"

Q17 – "Tell me about a problem you encountered and how you resolved it."

Tell them about a problem and how you resolved it…ideally how you, working with others resolved it. This is an indirect team question. Several things can be fleshed out in response. Some interviewees may err on the side of "I did" such and such, "I resolved by…, "If it weren't for me…". In advance you may want to have a scenario or two in you head and focus on how you were part of a group solution.

Q18 – "What interests you in this job?"

Again, a variant on previous questions – I want you to be prepared for nearly any similar question. As before do not struggle or you could be finished. It should be very clear to you why it's important that the company choose someone who has thought this through and has a chance of actually enjoying their work. Few candidates are adequately prepared to answer.

Another item I failed to mention. Do NOT fall into the trap of telling your audience why you want to run from your current position. You need to have two or three solid reasons why you would like the job based on what you understand the job to be. Accelerate your career, improve some aspect of the role, deepen your experience in a certain field, you enjoy the tasks as advertised, you really want to grow business. Come up with something. In fact, if you are not clear on why you would like to tackle the position, why would you want to pursue it? Money alone is never an answer you wish to give – even if implicit. Be clear on the reasons before you even waste everyone's time with an interview. Convey your points with conviction.

Q19 – "Why are you willing to leave your current role?"

This is the other side to the previous question. There are a few never-dos in your response. Under no circumstance talk about how bad your boss is, how fucked-up the company is, what tight-wads they are, even if true never, and I mean never, discuss ethical shortcomings in your current company unless it's a matter of public record. If you're leaving an Enron we get it. How many times I've heard a candidate wax holy in describing questionable practices at work and saying "I just couldn't work there". Do you think the candidate got the benefit of the doubt? Nope. The red flags fly and you're done! Even if there is truth in this subject don't go there! Ever!

Now that I've covered what not to do, here is what to do. Valid reasons for leaving through the ears of the interviewer are that you've really enjoyed your current role but you are trying to grow your career in a different direction and you see a fit between the present opportunity and your strengths. Emphasize all the great things you learned and how good the people were. What you are seeking in the position you are interviewing for is not an opportunity that you are likely to see with your existing employer. And here's the other thing – the lack of opportunity has nothing to do with their assessment of you it's just not in their business model. Turn the answer to this question toward the opportunity you see in the advertised position you are interviewing for. Case closed. Don't waffle, don't elaborate too much, close with a positive! Nothing kills an interview faster than revealing some psychological hurt. Nothing bolsters your chances more than great vision and positive intent! If you harbor sour grapes never reveal it.

Q20 – "Can you give us an example of how you influenced the outcome of an important decision at work? Tell us what that was and what happened."

Another team question. The focus in the question appears to you. It's not. Your answer needs to describe a team situation and how you worked with the team members by presenting an argument and gaining their support. Then it was the team that acted on it and the team that delivered results. Don't use the word "team" too often either. Try "We", "us", "together", all those lovely emotive words HR departments cultivate. You'll get the points and impress the prospective "team" that you are a "team player".

Q21 – "Have you ever been confronted with a situation at work that presented ethical conflict? If so, describe it for us"

"Yeah, my boss told me if I selected a certain contractor I would get a $25K bonus. I told him this would be absolutely unethical and I could not consider it. That turned out to be a brilliant move! He upped it to $75K! You should see my new pool. SWEET!" This is a bonehead question at best but gets asked too often. Either don't present anything or think of a gray area where you actually did the right thing. No drama here please!

Q22 – "How do you deal with an employee who is creating conflict in your department?"

"Fire them! Run them out like yesterday's garbage!" O.k. this is another team question. It should be intuitive that you are being assessed how well you endeavor to work with your department members to find out what the problem may be. If the issue can be overcome and the person regains composure stepping happily back into the role of contributing team member then you have helped to save the day. That needs to be part of the answer. So what happens if you and the focus of the issue cannot resolve anything? There are people who are prone to conflict. It needs to be pointed out that if the discord is not external but stems from the source then in fact removal may be an option in that case. Really this is your time to present both paths.

Q23 – "How do you motivate your employees?"

This one is a bit tricky. It seems straightforward but what the interviewer may be looking for will vary. I will give you my view. Paraphrase at will the message below. Most high performing people are motivated by an environment that allows them to have a meaningful impact in their work. Many staff positions today have tremendous oversight and approval requirements. I believe that providing people with the tools they need and the latitude to influence what they were hired to do goes a long way in motivating the right kind of employee. Birthday cakes, dinners, parties, and other forms of "atta-boys" are largely useless. If a department launches a successful platform, breaks a sales record, or surpasses some goal it's a great idea to celebrate but we're not talking about children here. They are not motivated by gimmicks. Performers are infinitely more fulfilled when they have the freedom and the resources to do what they were hired for. If you really want to motivate a high-performer try creating an environment where their pay is influenced by performance – right to the factory worker.

Few companies are this brave. How de-motivating it is to live in a "do-as-you-are-told" environment. High expectations and high reward potential, coupled with resources and the lack of micromanagement will motivate the right kind of person.

If a follow-up question probes motivating "not the right kind of person" your answer is simple. Creating the right environment will surface detractors and they can be weeded out. If someone needs the stick more than the carrot no one has the time for this.

Q24 – "What motivates you?"

Much the same thing as the aforementioned – you don't need to go into great detail here. Money goes without mention and shouldn't be used as an illustration other than to offer that you like part or your pay connected to your performance. Again, not all companies will honor your request but they will not be put off by your wish either. Suggest that you like the freedom and the tools to make a positive mark on the company you work for.

Q25 – "What would be your plans for the first 60 days on this job?"

Avoid talking about how you are going to change the department. To wax cliché, keep it real. The most important aspect of nearly any company is its people. Sounds tacky but that's the gist of it. In two months, realistically, if you spend time learning the people you will be working with and get started learning processes, customers, suppliers, and others you will be interacting with you're doing well. An answer focusing primarily on learning processes and functions will miss the HR point – it's the people that matter. Make sure you discuss this.

Q26 – "What about the first year?"

Everything mentioned before but now you've got time to really dig into the functionary aspects of your role. Realistically in a year you might have formulated more clearly how you will invoke change, leave your mark, or improve something about your department/company. A year, though, is hardly time to complete those processes. Again, I'd avoid promising the world. Your goal in your first year is to have a pretty solid understanding of your job and the people you will work with. Many will make the mistake when asked this question of declaring their intentions to alter the Universe.

Q27 – "Do you have any questions of us?"

"No, you sound like a great group of people to work with!" The next thing you'd hear is good bye! You'd better have some questions. Lean on your research. Before walking into this interview you already understood competitors, markets, market strategy, products, structure of the company etc. You will impress your audience heavily by asking questions that demonstrate your understanding of likely challenges. Put them on their heels a bit. Ask them how they plan to deal with a competitive expansion. What are their thoughts about dealing with a shrinking market? What are they doing to innovate? If they are a utility company what are they doing regarding operational efficiency? Why is there an opening for the position you are interviewing for? Do not miss this last question. Much needs to be learned about why a role is vacant.

This is your chance to turn the control of the interview over to you. It is also your time to sell your vision. My "Golden-Rule"...remember? Now you must ask leading questions about what the company hopes to achieve in hiring a new person for the advertised role. Questions such as "Aside from the duties you've described...how do you see a successful candidate impacting the profit-and-loss for the department?" If it's absurdly obvious, don't ask. Otherwise listen to them for a while. Next question you might ask. "What type of person would you consider the ideal candidate?" You might turn the time questions around on them..."What would you like to see out of a new candidate in the first year?" Finally, "What would you like to see from the department I am applying for?"

By now they might be ready for you to leave. Not without your closing the sale. So you've heard what they consider important. You have a message to give about what you would like to do for the department/division/company. Now would be the time. Share how you see the role and the impact you wish to have. Confirm with a question..."Am I far off the mark?" Assuming you are haven't run too far astray then continue describing the benefit you hope to bring - something novel maybe but show that you have thought through your strategy. Focus on how you will energize the "Team" to further the company's interests. Don't go too far out on a limb, remember, you've thought this through! You mapped it out. You are only telling it now.

Some rules in sharing your vision. It needs to be quick. No more than two minutes unless the interviewer(s) whish to engage in a Q & A. Ideally you are just hitting the outline but you are providing enough detail to whet their appetite. Obviously it needs to be real. You researched the company, potential impact of the target role, and you've built a plan regarding what you will bring to the role. Tell it well and close out.

General Considerations:

- ❖ In many roles your documented experience matters very little during the interview. Don't expect the interviewers to be at all familiar with your resume even though they've had a copy for the last week. Outline it for them verbally. This is usually best done at the beginning of the interview.
- ❖ Conventional wisdom is true – a successful interview has the interviewer talking at least 30% of the time. You will want to keep your answers enlightening but concise. Ask questions.
- ❖ In contrast to the structured environment interviewers are people. They are trying to find out how well you will "gel" with potential cohorts ("likeability index") and that you can do the job well. Added bonuses would include bringing additional success to the effort and that you mesh with the "culture".

❖ Opinions are formed quickly. True, you can blow an interview at any moment, but generally within five or ten minutes the interviewers will have a strong idea whether or not they want to move forward with you.

❖ Generally all candidates that make it to the interview will be "qualified" in a cursory sense to meet the needs of the job. Differentiation will be made via personality, preparation, and delivery in a superficial sense.

❖ Most candidates will show up without a plan.

❖ The likelihood of your winning with a plan as described earlier is high.

Dos and Don'ts:

Do Not…

❖ Convey any negativity – at all – ever! Got it? More often that you might believe, people assume an interview is an o.k. forum to reveal their, shall we say, "quirks".

❖ Assume the interviewers are your friends and appreciate your sense of humor. You will appear presumptuous at best and potentially stupid at worst.

❖ Talk too much or ramble.

❖ Talk too little or seem withdrawn.

❖ Circumvent questions or dodge questions – listen intently and provide your best direct answer.

❖ Interrupt.

❖ Be overly nervous – there's no need. You're prepared…remember? Focus on your story.

❖ Be defensive – again, you are primarily being

❖

❖ measured for how well you "gel" with potential co-workers.

❖ Assume any interviewer is familiar with your background because they received your resume.

- ❖ Bring copies and offer to review it with them. Highlighted points should relate to the opportunity in front of you.
- ❖ Ask about pay in the first interview.
- ❖ Use too much corporate jargon – examples include: "Think outside the box", "paradigm shift", "at the end of the day", "win-win", "low-hanging fruit", etc. Try English…it's refreshing. Your own words convey sincerity and novelty.
- ❖ Name drop. Assume in person that your connection "higher up" holds sway.
- ❖ Attempt a joke.
- ❖ Comment on the validity of an interview question – game over if you ever do!

In-person interview musts:

- ❖ Confirm time and place the day prior.
- ❖ Be slightly early (five to ten minutes and no more).
- ❖ Breath mints.
- ❖ Practice responses to Q1 – Q27. Of course there will be more but Q1 – Q27 and their variants are the crux of the discussion.
- ❖ Know your story! Know how to communicate the message of what you will do for this position and how that impacts profitability or the organization's goals.
- ❖ Dress appropriately. Know your audience and know your role. If you are not sure, then ask! It is o.k. to ask directly what manner of dress is most appropriate.
- ❖ Always, always, always, be positive and forthright.
- ❖ Be informative and concise.
- ❖ Always listen carefully to questions and scenarios.
- ❖ Thank each interviewer in writing (a.k.a. "hardcopy") after the interview! I always email each interviewer as well but hardcopy is a needed formality.

- ❖ Tell your story at the appropriate time.
- ❖ Inquire politely about the next step.
- ❖ Ask questions of your own! These should be to confirm market   direction, company vision, culture, those types of things.
- ❖ Be polite to everyone you meet on company premises.
- ❖ Answer directly and clearly each interview question.

Chapter Six – The Guts of the Matter

If you are out of work and looking, working but hoping for something better, or looking to move up in the company you are working for, your approach will be slightly different in each mentioned case to meet your goal. Notice I said slightly different. The general approach is forever the same. Nuance will be mentioned but as an add-on at the end of the chapter.

My recommended approach to help your career path is not quick. You will be asked to perform methodical research, market yourself, and sell your vision. The necessary parts to your plan include: 1) Knowing what you have to offer and how that will benefit someone. 2) Understanding where the corresponding opportunities are. 3) Gaining access to the people who would be most influential in helping you. 4) Selling your message – describing how you will help your target organization. 5) Securing the job and setting yourself up for continued success.

The first step should be the easiest. If you have a specific degree and professional licensure it truly isn't that hard but for the rest of us it may be more difficult to write down in a short sentence what you would like to do for someone else in the next five years and more importantly how they will benefit. As a start, why the hell do you work? Beyond making a living, what do you have to offer the world? Now is the time to take counsel and figure out where you think you would benefit perspective employers the most. I want to discourage the notion, with rare exception, that each of us has some perfect fit in the world. Tough love, you most likely don't. Most activities representing meaningful work contain drudgery, boredom, tedium, frustration, attention to detail, disappointment, and conflict. The fulfillment comes in looking back over your accomplishments knowing you weathered those storms to help you and your employer reach a goal.

I'm basically telling you to drop the romantic idea that there is some holistic activity that will satisfy you on a spiritual level. What is important to you is less critical than what is important to a potential employer. The trick here is to assess what you can do for someone else. It should be within your capacity, obviously. You don't have to be an expert or even necessarily deeply trained. You must, though, identify the good you will bring someone else and write it down! Think of it this way, if each of us were truly a contractor, what would you offer companies so that they could become more valuable? What would they pay you the most for? For most of us that is a functional thing. Maybe you can increase sales for a company, bring product or process design expertise, offer better health-care support, perhaps you have a knack for navigating the morass of regulatory laws and keeping a company compliant. You have training, perhaps formal education, and experience that will benefit someone. As a foot-note I seldom encourage wholesale career changes after age thirty-five. At least in a loose way, stick to what you are good at and build from there. Your career may morph as you ascend but enhancing what you are good at has more value and can more quickly lead to something you enjoy than a spiritual epiphany that entirely redirects your career forcing you to start all over.

I leave the burden with you to figure out the what. The first step of the plan, though, is to write the benefit statement down. That's not the benefit to you…that's the benefit to someone else. Notice the "customer-focus" here? Think of the posture change. Those in demand, good times and bad, are genuinely concerned in helping someone else. When you are a customer you gladly part with your money for good service and gnash your teeth at bad. Self-focus makes service difficult.

O.k. So step one is finished. You now have identified what you wish to offer and the benefit it will provide someone. Now the work begins. As a second step I mentioned finding out where you can successfully offer your services. You may already know. If you don't, then you have some research to do. No advice here really. If you truly understand your offerings then make a list of all the organizations you can think of that would benefit the most and offer you the most opportunity. To help you manage your time and have the best chance of success, choose three to start.

Combining steps one and two you now need to write a specific benefit statement aimed at your target companies.

Your benefit statement needs to be something you are convinced you will do for someone. Something specific - examples:

1) Help Mini-Parts Industries penetrate the medical device market for their micro-machined products.
2) Grow ZZ Instrumentation's presence in the OEM markets by selling applications to the appliance industry.
3) Help to bolster City Hospital's image as a premium patient care facility by raising expectations of the nursing staff.
4) Help to cut operating expenses for Company N by optimizing supply-chain logistics for the Scooter Project.
5)   Use my operations experience to boost quality for the coffee-maker line and cut costs.
6) Increase Chamber membership by 20%.

Audacity, balls, gumption - how in the hell can you assert such? You need to have a plan and be able to explain it well. It does not have to be perfect nor do you need every detail. You do need an outline that makes sense. Bragging though it will seem, you will be given an audience if you can back it up! I'm not asking you to lie. After you've assessed an organization's needs and understand how your goals help meet their objective(s) tie the two together and tell it.

Step three, gaining access to decision makers, is most challenging when you are not employed or do not know much about target organizations. In the case where you are trying to enhance your career with the company you now work for you still have to do the work but gaining access to the right people should be easy. I'll address the most difficult case.

Let's assume you don't know anyone who can help you in a target organization and you need to find someone. A company will only reveal what it wants to on its company website so that may give you some cursory information but not a lot more. There are, however, public records of products and services a company has that you can access on line. For example, suppose your goal is to be a mechanical engineer in product design for a consumer products company. Why not look up their patents online at www.uspto.gov? You will find the names of inventors. Likely they assigned their invention to their employer but you will have access to the names of anyone having inventorship disclosed in a utility patent. Call them. Assuming they are still at the company you can then follow the chain to find out who would be the hiring manager for mechanical engineers. This is a "back-door" method. Sometimes the front desk will answer the question for you.

Let me also address Step 3 (gaining access to decision makers) in two categories. One instance would be where a target company is posting a position you want. The second subcategory would be where you are trying to sell you way into an organization without a posting. In the first case, where you are trying to reach the hiring manager and the position is posted, HR is typically serving as a screen. You may as well submit your information to the public posting but the odds of your resume and cover-letter reaching a decision maker are slim. My advice is to send your information through human resources anyway but you need to do more. You will want to try the front desk and ask to speak to someone managing the department in which you are applying. If you explain yourself well you've got about a thirty percent chance of having the receptionist put your call through if you have no name. If you cannot find the name on Google or through company news or any other public venue then here is what you do. Someone you know knows someone working for the target company. I'll nearly guarantee it. Begin your quest. Literally ask anyone you can think of if they know someone working for the company…even if it's a different branch. This needs to be someone who will vouch for you. You need a mole. Once you have a name you will need to call this person and have them research it from the "inside" for you. You're not asking anything highly confidential…simply the name of someone high enough in the right part of the organization who will at least know the person making the hiring decision. That is your "in".

In the second case, where you are not responding to a posting but you want to sell your way into a company you will want to present your idea as high up the organizational chart as you can. Who this is will depend on the size of the company. If small, it needs to be the president/CEO...good news is that person will be easy to find. If you are calling an organization with 5,000 people and you want a staff job you will never hurt yourself by starting high and having your information passed down several layers but I will advise you to take a more realistic approach. In this case assess the level you are trying for and find someone at least at the level who will hire you...obviously. Don't make a judgment error and sell yourself to a peer – won't work. Building an organizational chart from the outside isn't too hard once you've done it a few times. Again, friends, relatives, co-workers, someone knows someone who works at your target company. They can easily give you names. Never deal with anyone dense enough to direct inquiries to HR when you are trying to sell a proposition to someone. I will address how to sell your message shortly. When you succeed in finding someone who will listen to your pitch, your message needs to grab their attention – you will get one shot. More on that later – the point here is that it's not too hard to find people from the outside if you have time.

If you are trying to create opportunity within your present organization you have a much easier (albeit you must be patient) task. It simply comes down to the whole "networking" thing within the company. Be visible, schedule meetings with people who can influence your direction, let your supervisor know what your long-term goals are, all of those common-sense things, but you have the company roster at your disposal.

Let's review. You roughly know what you want to sell, you've identified organizations that need you – either through their postings or your research, and you've uncovered the names of those you need to sell your message to. We're now in step four. The sell will be happen differently for a posted position than in the case of you trying to create an opportunity. The time-frame will be the most notable difference.

I'll refer you to Chapter Five and my message on interviewing if you are trying to sell your message to an audience relative to a posted position.

Now, to the case where you are about to contact a company having no stated personnel needs – "life is good" as far as they know. Contacting business leaders in the organizations and conveying any uncertainty in your message would be tantamount to closing a door forever. Your message needs to show profit. Your earlier crafted benefit statement will need to be refined. In this case you are proposing a business service to help the organization make money. In the event you are a non-profit then perhaps your message needs to illustrate how you will grow membership. On that premise you will further propose that the best way for them to profit is to create a position and hire you. I never said this was simple. What I can tell you is that this avenue is so seldom considered that when executed well your chances for success are huge. But you truly need to have something to offer and it can't be vague.

So, how are you going to sell? Here is my approach. I draft a well-written letter to the individual you have identified. This opens with some variant of your benefit statement. If you are proposing to increase a manufacturing line output, you need to identify which line, by how much, roughly how you propose doing it (omitting some detail), and what gives you the qualifications to back it up. If it's a marketing job you are after you will explain how you intend to position a product to gain share over a named competitor(s). Just the audacity of the letter will intrigue. You're letter needs to be concise, factual, and omit enough detail that he will want to know more. You mention also that you will be in touch by phone within four or five days.

Understanding mid-to-high-level professionals have numerous competing priorities you will be patient, polite, yet persistent in your efforts to call. If your call is neither returned nor answered within a week or so you may need to try another avenue. If, however, the phone is answered then don't be shocked. Brevity and to the point in your introduction will be critical. You name, the reason for your call, ask if the person has a few minutes, and support your point.

Let's work an example that covers the process through the call. Let's suppose your goal is to manage a sales team selling a product line your company does not offer. You have been in technical sales for over seven years. You've been successful but you believe there is a line of industrial products sold by another company that your company will never be involved with. In fact, you are not even a competitor in the least. In your career you believe you've uncovered application potential that is enormous and not being considered by the company producing the product line. To further clarify the example let's say the product is some type of emission control device used in the utility market but you see tons of potential working with industrial clients. The device is used on coal-fired boilers for power generation. You understand the potential application and you've researched the product line to the point that you could alter the product slightly and make it work for the applications you've identified. You have a vision to grow sales. You will want to do your own marketing research and quantify the potential. You will also develop an outline of how you would manage a sales force to grow product sales. You will need to outline why you are the person that could best do that. Remember, you have sold products – you've never managed a sales force so you will have to address this.

Your benefit statement could be constructed something like this. "My goal is to triple revenue for the pollution control retrofit market within five years by expanding the market to industrial gas-fired, coal, black liquor, and oil-fired boiler systems." You now need to build the framework of a business plan to support the benefit statement. Call decision makers in the industrial base to find out what they currently use if anything and understand the level of urgency to install something in light of pending air-permit changes. This should also give you some sense of the margin potential. You will want to make a wild guess at how much such a device would cost to produce. This is a lot of work. No kidding.

But assuming you really want to do this, you will need to demonstrate you've thought this through. This is where most people fall apart. The world is replete with ideas and short on sweat equity. Those who succeed are long on the latter.

So now you have your plan, your benefit statement, and you need to know who you should talk to in the target organization. You call, you ask friends, and finally a customer of yours has a business card of an individual from another division in the target company. You call and introduce yourself explaining that you would like to propose an idea to someone in the target division. He knows an engineer. You call the engineer, he figures out you are trying to get a job with the company and gives you the number for human resources. You're finished, right? This is where you need to be bold. Your vision is bold. You have produced a business plan and no mid-level manager will want to take the time to understand the benefit. You need to call the CEO or someone in the top tier. No harm will be done. Trust me on this example. You are talking about new markets and revenue growth. Big stuff.

CEOs are easy to find. Check the company news on the website, use Google, the top person is easy to find. Success! After running through company news you find the name for the COO, Marla Blevins, instead. You call Marla's secretary. Here's how it goes...oh! And your name is Roger Hamilton for this exercise. "Marla Blevins' office, this is Trisha."

"Hi Trisha, my name is Roger Hamilton. I have a business proposal for Ms. Blevins that I would like to present..." Ooops. You've already died. Trisha's role is the screener from hell. She is paid to deflect all but relevant calls. You will need to be direct and pointed with Trisha. Let's try honesty. Assuming she just gave the pat introduction your response this time is different.

"Hi Trisha, my name is Roger Hamilton. I would like to talk to Ms. Blevins about growing your combustion pollution control business. I've identified a way to do this that I'd like to talk with her about."

"Sir, who are you with?"

"I am representing myself today. I know this sounds a bit weird. I work in an unrelated field and I've got insight into markets I'm not sure she's considered – markets that your products would really benefit."

"Sir, let me get your name and a number where I can have her call you back. She's busy today."

"Fair enough – in the meantime would you mind if I emailed her my contact information as well?"

This may be the best you can do on first pass but Marla Blevins will at least get the note. Her assistant is not stupid. She too understands that you are talking about helping the company. If you can ever thread a personal note into the call with the assistant you can gain an ally. Likely you'll have an email address too. I've had variants of this conversation often both as a sales person and prospecting for new work. The phone will ring or at a minimum you will see a reply on your email. Once done you will not want to further this conversation via email. Obviously you will want to talk directly. You have her ear. She is at least intrigued. Now you've got to lay it out for her. You will have to be detailed but not give her the recipe. Let's suppose you now get through to Marla directly.

"Hi, Ms. Blevins, this is Roger Hamilton. I want to thank you first for your time and also for your willingness to hear my ideas…"

A COO will want a Reader's Digest version initially. Focus on the benefit.

"…I love your product line for pollution control on utility boilers for the power industry. My research says this is about a $150MM/year market – is that close?"

"Not too far off, go ahead, what can you do for us?"

"In the last seven years I have become quite familiar with key heavy industrial markets, and with a slight adaptation to your systems, I think you have a $300MM/year market right in front of you with margin potential in the 45% - 55% range. I would like to share with you how you could grow this market."

"Mr. Hamilton, we already have our engineers looking into this market. We are quite aware of the potential."

"With all due respect, I don't doubt that, after all you run a great company. Where I think I can help, however, is get your engineers in front of key decision makers in the oil & gas industry, paper, primary metals, and chemical processing. In fact, placing your engineers with the right people can collapse your time-frame in capturing this market before your competitor captures market share. To be pointed, I think I can open the doors that will allow you to have 80% of this market locked up within five years."

Think she may be interested?

"O.k. what company did you say you were with?"

"Ms. Blevins, I am interested in working directly for you. I would like to manage a sales team focused on brining this market to you."

You've brought the fish to the bait. The rest if filling in the blanks. Naturally Marla will want to know why you? She will want to know how in the hell you came up with this epiphany, but it doesn't really matter – does it? She wants to grow her company and you hold a key to help. Nice work. Your pay, your future position, the terms, in her mind those are only details if you've secured the strategy.

Remember, this is one example. All fields are not the same but you will want to follow the path in much the same way. Yes it's work on your behalf. But guess what? If you are not willing to go into that level of detail then it's unlikely you are the type of person who will move yourself upwards. It takes initiative but no more than would be expected in your job. So seldom do people apply themselves in the most critical aspect of their careers – defining what they want to do and selling it to the right people. There is a general mind-set that if you exist and get good reviews at work, people will want you. Absolute crap! You will need to become good at selling your ideas. It's not that hard because the sales efforts by most of your would-be competitors isn't there. Most candidates would never consider creating their own opportunity.

Even if your field does not directly impact markets or sales you can apply a similar strategy. If your goal is to join the accounting department of a health-services company you probably don't want to call on the CEO. Again, though, you will want to write down your plan on how you intend to improve accounting practices at the company and then consider who you should contact. The benefit you intend to articulate will determine who you need to talk to. If your goal is to help this health services company better comply with Sarbanes-Oxley you may want to start with a division controller. Draft your benefit statement (you may want to research the company via someone on the inside to confirm they need help with compliance practice). Describe to the controller why you are the person to help move the accounting department toward better compliance. Pretty gutsy – not behavior you will find often. Sell your vision to the controller and there may be no need for a formal interviewing process. You are likely in if he is sold. The chief benefit to you is this – fulfill your vision, deliver what you promised and the likelihood of promotion is almost absolute. You are not a "staff" worker, a controlled expense, a run-of-the-mill piece-of-shit forsaking the least effort to draw a paycheck. The world still rewards those with vision and execution. Be that person.

Chapter Seven – Loose Ends

Work is what you do the majority of your life. Work is the most hated, feared, needed, controversial, depressing, annoying, stressful, confusing, facet of your life. The only thing worse is being without it. It becomes your identity. Make sure you choose a rewarding path.

Post World War II until mid-2008 the United States was a nation where goals centered around furthering our material position were reasonable. "Globalization" and mismanagement of finance (both individual and in particular in government) introduces a dynamic from which we are not immune. Travel to Korea, China, Latin America, Eastern Europe and take a close look at the standard of living. Consider the fact that people living in those countries are equally viable to do your job. Any guesses where your standard of living may be headed? The decades to follow will see an "equalization" in global standards of living. To be sure, it's not a net-sum-zero game...aggregate wealth will increase but forces on salaries and currency value will not play in your favor.

That's the bad news. As with any challenge you need to understand it and deal with it. The need to work in some fashion will not go away. Paucity of conventional opportunity will create panic. You need to seize control rather than be a passive participant in this mess. Commerce will not cease. Distribution of food and durable goods will not cease. Obviously GNP and just about any measure of production will not be great news but we still demand beer, toilet paper, tooth-paste, pet-food, clothing, autos on a less aggressive schedule, doctor's visits, movies, furnishings, toys, and so on. It will slow but it won't go away.

What have you learned in the previous chapters? I hope you now understand how to network, research positions, answer hard-hitting interview questions, follow-up, create your own opportunities, and a little bit about selling yourself. As a people it is our nature to be driven to materially enhance our positions in life. This won't quit either. Forget about the lunatic fringe equating developing circumstances as a call to live a more holistic life. That's not the silver lining in this cloud. They were smoking plenty of dope during the good times and that won't change in the bad (aside from running out of money – home grown will likely be a burgeoning industry).

You might want to step back, assess what you are after and execute on the advice I've given you. It's worked for many – I count my blessings each day that someone as mundane and stupid as I am is blessed with opportunity during slow times.

Invariably the most common questions I am asked focus on how to approach people who may hold a key to prospective opportunity. In written and in spoken form how do you reach out to people who can help? I touched on this in Chapters Four and Five but given the import perhaps more attention is merited. Examples and templates may be most helpful.

Let's assume for this discussion that you have identified who you are going to call on. Further, you have clearly identified in your mind what you will do for them. In this example you are in supply-chain logistics (fancy for "buyer") and your company is dying. Your research surfaced a growing agricultural business. You've identified the CEO and you want to position yourself as a purchasing manager. You've never managed more than a few people as a senior buyer but you think what you've learned can help the target company. You are aware that the target company, let's call it "Ag-Flo", is trying to expand in arenas that would have them buying chemicals and tanks that you are very familiar with. Your first introduction ought to be in writing to stage a call you will make a few days after Ag-Flo's receipt of your superbly-written letter. Your name is "Jessica Mendez".

The letter:

Jessica Mendez
4545 45th Street
Slowtown, GA 12345
(123) 543-9876
Jessica.m@gobblydgook.com

August 22, 2010

Mr. George Patterwomp
President and CEO
Ag-Flo Corporation
Someothertown, TN 23433

Re: Supply-chain optimization proposal

Dear Mr. Patterwomp:

My name is Jessica Mendez. I would like to help Ag-Flo Corporation realize profit-growth that more closely tracks your year-over-year revenue growth. You have now reached business volume that would allow you to gain a much better cost position relative to tank assemblies and "proprietary" chemicals. In total these costs present a large portion of your operating expense. I can help. Two of your key suppliers are companies I work with and have helped to negotiate long-term contracts cutting 40% of related unit cost.

I would like to call you early next week to see if you would be open to meeting in person for further discussion. I am currently employed at DCY Corporation and feel my interests and abilities would better serve Ag-Flo. I would like to present a plan to you that may increase your profit margins upwards of 5%. My contact information is provided above in the event you wish to contact me in the interim. My thanks in advance for your consideration.

Best regards,

Jessica Mendez

Key points. You (Jessica) offered nothing, absolutely nothing about specific work or education background that would apply to a "job". Note the departure from tradition and this is the basis of this book. You stated the benefit. You researched the company. You have a **plan**!!! My question…putting yourself in George Patterwomp's shoes, do you think you might be interested to discuss this? Again, this approach may strike some as arrogant. Quit it! It's not. In factual terms you are offering to help Mr. Patterwomp make more money.

If this blows up into a requisition for a purchasing manager and the usual postings etc. are to follow, who holds the advantage? You basically write the deal and the rest is formality – simply details.

I have written dozens of letters similar to the above. They need to be short, informative, polite, and absolutely state the benefit in clear terms. Note that you/Jessica did not say how you were going to get there. That's not important…yet. There was some reference to having worked with two of the suppliers before but details need to be left out of the initial communiqué. If you were a waiter but knew how to pull off a deal like this the CEO would be interested. Another great benefit to this approach is that it clears the deck for the usual stupid analysis of who is most qualified.

Now I've left you with a concrete example of how you might approach a prospect in written form. To carry this example further you've promised a phone call. You need to make it…and by the way, you will be put through. Nearly guaranteed.

Without scripting the phone call Mr. Patterwomp will have some key questions. He will be interested to know why you have identified Ag-Flo as a company to work for. You now understand you answer these questions by emphasizing what you feel you can do for Ag-Flo and how you think this might lead to a great mutual relationship. Say nothing about the swan dive your company is likely to take or lead the conversation in a direction that focuses on you. Express your belief that you are uniquely positioned to help

Ag-Flo become more competitive allowing you to orchestrate the efforts of a purchasing department.

Mr. Patterwomp may want you to reveal in detail how you intend to exact your battle plans. Request a meeting to review. You are not interested in giving him a step-by-step roadmap but if he's truly interested in your services then the two of you need to meet.

To wrap up this example, you are now in a position to make use of the interview approaches outlined in previous chapters. The intent of this example was to provide detail regarding how you trigger interest to start the conversation.

Comments on Resumes

You noticed I have not said much about the resume. It should be clear why not. From past discussion did a resume ever win the day? Do you know this is the least-considered piece of information in a candidate search? Traditionally it had merit. Today it has almost none. Consider a resume necessary but woefully insufficient. What I've tried to tell you in so many ways is contemporary winners in the job-search game have sold themselves in one way or another – quite often long before a resume is presented.

Think about the resume. If you've worked for more than four years this is a horribly inadequate means of communicating your value and you are depending on some overtaxed human resources contact knowing enough to accurately profile you based on sketchy information and an assumed desire to read it in the first place. Again, you will need to produce a resume in any search but if you've followed the advice in this book the resume becomes no more than a formality. I will discuss how to prepare it.

In an anonymous job search you will need to play the game of buzz-words. Put yourself in the role of this mythical HR person and what do you do trying to fill a requisition? Assuming further that filling the job is not pre-ordained, you will receive hundreds of inquiries for a good opportunity. Your job is to take some slice of your packed day and screen ten or so candidates from a massive pile. First-pass review will not allow for a full read of each. A cursory glance at key words, similar background, and perhaps education will be all that time allows.

As a candidate you will need to customize a resume for every job to which you apply for if you are only to pursue careers via the traditional path – everything I've been arguing against. However, there is one lesson I want you to learn in resume writing. Quite simply, even with the sales effort you will assemble, you will want to speak to the job or opportunity you are vying for. Stupidly obvious, right? Should be yet again, so few engage in this manner. Again, for emphasis, if you've done all that you need to up front there is a real chance you will be at your first interview without anyone having actually read the document. They will have a copy but you will need to review your history using it as a vague outline. A two or three page resume will never alone sell much of anything.

Back to the subject here are a few pointers:

❖ I do encourage a resume to open with an objective statement. This point is debated often. Many feel this should be discarded as no one cares what you are looking for. I agree! Yet in so stating they've overlooked another message to be communicated in an objective statement – the benefit statement to the prospective employer. That is how you write an objective statement. You state your desire to help an organization do something. Examples will follow.

❖ One to three pages in length. For some time there was a goal to keep your career to a single page. Good luck! No harm in two pages. If you must add a third keep it brief.

❖ My favorite format from top to bottom is: Objective Statement, Professional Summary (highlights from your entire career), Professional History (the traditional reverse chronology), Formal Education, Professional Associations/Licensure/Etc.

❖ For Christ Sake do NOT add family members, hobbies, church affiliations, anything quaint. Sorry have to belabor the obvious but I see this too often.

❖ In the second section entitled "Professional Summary" you will tailor each version of your resume to address a target opportunity. This is the buzzwords section. You need to sell yourself quickly here.

❖ Always have an updated "base copy". Should the need arise you can then customize within minutes.

❖ Have someone with decent linguistic ability proof-read your resume. No detractors allowed on this not-so-important formality. You still can't afford to screw it up.

Discussion and examples:

You may want to consider placing your contact information on the header of each page or at least the top of the first...

"Bernard Simpson

123 First Street, Birmingham, AL 31347 • (205) 123-4567 • Bernard.simpson@foofoo.com"

Next item...the objective statement!

"Objective: To help drive the growth and profitability of a customer-focused company through successful application of account management or operations management."

Very vanilla but you can tailor this to be specific to your opportunity. For example, let's suppose you are going to sell industrial equipment to Latin America...

"Objective: Grow product market share in Latin America for a fast-pace industrial company supported by my fluency in Spanish and Portuguese and contact base in South America and Mexico."

If you cannot provide a specific related benefit, then by all means drop it.

Next item…Professional Summary or simply "Summary". Example –

"Summary:

⇨ Management of domestic and foreign OEM accounts representing $50MM annual revenue.
⇨ Negotiated long-term contracts with key OEM customers.
⇨ Managed new product-development projects supporting $7MM annual OEM sales.
⇨ Managed project teams to relocate domestic manufacturing to Mexico supporting $40MM in annual revenue and $4.5 MM in added annual operating income contribution.
⇨ Drafted and championed capital requisitions up to $25MM."

Again, this part ought to be tailored to the opportunity you are chasing. The next section is obviously your work history in reverse chronology. You are on your own here. The only thing I will mention is that the conventional wisdom of beginning with action words such as "managed", or "sold", or "developed" is appropriate. Everyone does this nowadays.

Under education, the next section, you may want to elaborate if you feel there is some aspect to your education and training that will help you support your message. Otherwise this is dry and perfunctory.

The last segment of the resume is to list out any of your professional trade associations, licenses, and additional training. Now you are done.

Again, rarely does anyone end up with a job based on the resume. The rare cases may be if you are one of only two or three people qualified for a very specific job and only a handful of resumes are submitted then perhaps you have an "in". Spoken to exhaustion, if you research, sell your message (the benefit statement), interview well, the resume will simply be a good coaster during the interview. You must have one but other than making it speak to the opportunity and keeping it current as a subject it's terribly overplayed in most "get a job" advice books.

Winding down

For those who like the "Here's what I am going to say-now I'm saying it-this is what I just said" approach I'd like to briefly touch on the key points again. In the same way a preacher pounds the same points repetitively until the brain either accepts or is forced into submission there are aspects to a job search in the beleaguered economy you must engage to reach your goals.

With the traditional approach still in practice but absurdly non-productive the burden to sell yourself rests with you and forever will. Not that this is bad. This gives you the opportunity to study and understand what you want and how you will benefit someone. Tying the two together via research you will uncover meaningful opportunity and then craft your message to sell the benefit. Through written and spoken media you will communicate the benefit, briefly the means, but most importantly the plan on how you will impact the fortunes of your target opportunity hence the company. The plan is vital. Inasmuch as this is real you will begin your new job with direction. Instead of looking to your superiors for marching orders, you wrote them. Live up to your expectations and deliver what you promised…if you fall short, adjust your plan and keep trying.

As you move through your career make key contacts and nurture relationships as these become the conduits to opportunity. Work your career well and this will serve you. Advertise your success appropriately as you will be remembered should free-agency be your calling. Take care of your body, your finances, and spend some amount of time improving you. You are a complete package – market yourself. That's more easily done when you can be proud of your appearance and what you offer.

Opportunity has forever changed. Only fools will count on human resources to connect the dots between their documented history and a position HR is ill-equipped to understand. You must be the selling agent. You must identify and make the contacts. You must identify how you can help. You must propose a plan. Finally, you must work the plan. Scary? Shouldn't be. Few follow these rules. It's not that hard. For at least another five years or so most will passively submit their background information to roles that are only potentially related to their background. If you are driving the process you can move your career in directions of your choosing.

I trust you enjoyed the book and found it of use. I invite you to use the advice and contact me. Let me know how it worked for you. Hearing and learning the experience of others helps me to improve my understanding of the process as well. My best to you planning your career!

www.ingramcontent.com/pod-product-compliance
Lightning Source LLC
Chambersburg PA
CBHW071227170526
45165CB00003B/1021